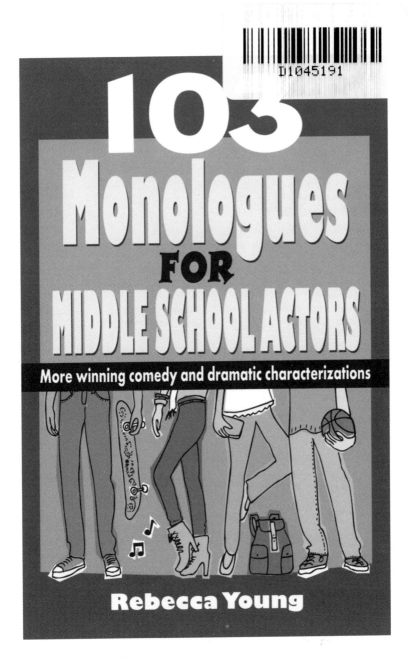

103

Monologues

FOR

MIDDLE SCHOOL ACTORS

More winning comedy and dramatic characterizations

Rebecca Young

MERIWETHER PUBLISHING LTD.
Colorado Springs, Colorado

Meriwether Publishing Ltd., Publisher
PO Box 7710
Colorado Springs, CO 80933-7710

www.meriwether.com

Editor: Theodore O. Zapel
Assistant editor: Nicole Deemes
Cover design: Jan Melvin

Library of Congress Cataloging-in-Publication Data

Young, Rebecca, 1965-
  103 monologues for middle school actors : more winning comedy and dramatic
characterizations / by Rebecca Young. -- First edition.
      pages cm
  ISBN 978-1-56608-194-8 (pbk.)
1. Monologues. 2. Dialogues. 3. Acting. I. Title. II. Title: One
hundred three monologues for middle school actors. III. Title: One
hundred and three monologues for middle school actors.
  PN2080.Y666 2013
  812'.6--dc23

                                        2013029803

          1   2   3   13   14   15

This book is dedicated to my awesome family: Heather, Kristina, Ashley, Chris, and to my new future family: Beau, Jordan, Landen, and all the Wrights.

Thanks for the inspiration for 103 more monologues — make sure to look for characters that may or may not sound just like you!

Here's to new beginnings, fun, laughter, and love.

Contents

Introduction

When I started this journey of writing yet another hundred plus monologues, I thought I could never do it. I didn't think there was any topic I'd left untouched thus far. But it's amazing how many middle school memories come flooding back either through my own crazy school days, or stories told by friends, family, or complete strangers! I guess that's because those middle school years are so unforgettable for most of us.

Hopefully you'll find a monologue in this bunch that speaks to you. With 103 to choose from, there's sure to be one that takes hold and doesn't let go. So take some time to find just the right one, and then make it your own. Want to make your class die laughing? Or bring them to tears? It's up to you! Good luck and break a leg!

1. Princess Pampering

(Girl)

1   I know there are some things in life that you are
2   supposed to outgrow. Like wearing underwear that has the
3   days of the week on them. Or Velcro sneakers so that you
4   don't have to learn how to tie. Or thinking that there are
5   monsters under your bed, or in your closet, or outside your
6   window. Or even thinking that you can fly like Peter Pan. Of
7   course you're supposed to outgrow things like that.
8   But some things we're forced to give up that we really
9   shouldn't. Why can't I want to be a princess? With beautiful
10 gowns and a handsome prince and a beautiful castle with
11 lots and lots of servants and absolutely no chores? It's not
12 completely impossible, right? I mean, there *are* still princes
13 and princesses in the world. Hello! What about Prince
14 Charles? And Prince William? And the beautiful Princess
15 Kate? *She* became a princess, didn't she? She was just an
16 everyday, normal, average girl like me when she was
17 growing up! I bet her parents and friends and teachers
18 didn't tell *her* she couldn't grow up to be a princess! Well,
19 maybe they did, but look how wrong they were!
20   So here's the thing. I'm going to Disney World next week
21 for spring break, and I've been saving my money for months
22 so that for one day, I can be treated like a princess. I'm
23 talking hair, clothes, makeup — the works! When I walk
24 around that park, I am going to be Cinderella for the whole
25 day. I've been practicing how to wave and smile and walk
26 like a princess. I know it's silly for a girl my age to spend
27 her money on something so juvenile, but I've wanted to be
28 a princess since the very first fairy tale my grandmother

1   read to me.

2   If you're being honest with yourself, you probably want
3   to be one too! A life of glamour and pampering. People bow
4   down to you, for goodness' sake! And even though no one
5   will bow down to me at the park, think of all the little girls
6   who will be so excited to see me! I'll be a celebrity! They may
7   even ask for my autograph. Isn't that worth a few months of
8   allowance? I say it is! So don't look at me with those
9   judgmental eyes. In just one week, this girl here is going to
10 be a princess!

2. Detention for This?

(Girl or Guy)

1 *(The whole time the student is performing, he or she should*
2 *be tapping a pencil against a table, the wall, parts of the body*
3 *like a leg, etc.)*
4   I have no idea what just happened! There I was minding
5 my own business, not hurting a fly, and then bam! I'm
6 jerked out of my seat and escorted to the hallway! Like one
7 of those kids that back-talks the teachers, or sleeps in
8 class, or maybe even like that one kid who carved his name
9 in the top of his desk with a nail file! Things like this don't
10 happen to me! I'm the *good* kid. The straight A student.
11 The one who *always* does the homework. I'm the kid with
12 perfect attendance. I haven't missed a day of school in four
13 years now.
14   How am I going to face my parents? They're going to be
15 so disappointed. My brother is the one who gets the teacher
16 notes. The Saturday detentions. The bad grades. The
17 parent calls from other students saying that Andrew is
18 picking on them. They don't expect to get bad news about
19 me!
20   I don't even know what to tell them! I swear I don't even
21 understand what I did. I was just sitting there. Thinking
22 about the project Mrs. Fink had just assigned ... planning
23 out my poster board in my mind ... It was going to be epic!
24 I envisioned making the pictures look 3-D. I'd just read an
25 article on how you can do that by layering the pictures.
26   She says she asked me to stop. She says I just ignored
27 her and kept on doing it! Doing what? That's what I'd like
28 to know! I don't even remember her speaking to me. I guess

1   I was kind of in a daze. But is that a crime? Lots of kids
2   don't pay attention in class. Why would she jerk me out of
3   the chair that way? I didn't even think she was allowed to do
4   that! Especially when I didn't even do anything ... *(Stops and*
5   *stares at the pencil he or she has been tapping.)*
6   Oh, wait ... now I get it ... *(Knocks on door.)* Mrs. Fink ...
7   I'm sorry ...

3. Football Fouls

(Guy)

1 How am I supposed to tell the coach that I'm not sure
2 I'm cut out to be on the football team? He won't understand,
3 and it's not like I can tell him the truth. He'll think I'm being
4 ridiculous. No one quits the team for something like this. He
5 knows it's not because I can't play. I'm the fastest
6 quarterback this school has ever seen. Maybe even any
7 school in the county. Probably wouldn't be exaggerating to
8 say that I am the fastest in the state. So he'll know it isn't
9 because I'm intimidated to play ... or worse, afraid to sit the
10 bench. He'd never buy that.
11   He knows I love football too. I've been playing ever since
12 I can remember. Guess that's because my dad was a big
13 hero when it came to football back in high school. Everyone
14 knows he couldn't wait to have a son to toss the old pigskin
15 with. I think everyone in this town knows how much my
16 whole family adores the game. I don't think we've missed a
17 high school game since my father played there himself. His
18 alma mater. Where I will be playing next year when I get to
19 high school myself.
20   I want to make my dad proud and I know in one sense
21 my decision would make him proud because my parents are
22 very strict when it comes to acting like a gentleman and not
23 some foul-mouthed heathen. But can I really tell my coach
24 and my dad that I want to quit football because I can't stand
25 the locker room talk? It's downright filthy! These boys know
26 more cuss words than I've heard in my life. It's disturbing.
27 I wish I could block it out. Not let it get to me. But it's
28 nonstop. I literally counted the bad words yesterday — a

1   hundred and fifty in fifteen minutes! That's ten a minute.
2   Doesn't that seem excessive? And if it's this bad in middle
3   school, I'm sure it's a hundred times worse in high school!
4   Have none of these kids ever had soap put in their mouth?
5   I bet it wasn't like this back when my dad was playing. I bet
6   those guys had more respect for each other ... and for the
7   game! My dad would never have talked like this! He'll be
8   shocked to hear what the locker room has turned into. I
9   won't even have to figure out a way to quit — he'll probably
10 call the coach and quit for me! Just wait 'til I get home and
11 tell him ...

4. The Singing Social Studies Teacher

(Girl or Guy)

1   My teacher has gone stark raving mad. I'm not kidding.
2 He's really flipped his lid. He didn't start out this way either.
3 Up until this week, he was your normal, run-of-the-mill
4 teacher who taught us like all the other normal teachers.
5 You know, boring lectures, notes on the board, multiple
6 choice tests — the standard stuff we all get used to year
7 after year after year. I mean, he did do some things
8 differently, like play *Cash Cab* to help us learn random facts
9 and show us these homemade videos of historical places he
10 visited that were kind of cool because they weren't just
11 pictures in a book but actual video of places I may never
12 see. And he'd act silly in them, which made them a whole
13 lot more interesting than the stuff I've seen on the History
14 Channel. But even with the all that, he still seemed normal
15 ... more or less.
16   Then, we started the sixties era this week. And the dude
17 has gone crazy! Maybe it has something to do with all that
18 hippie stuff. You know, peace and love and all that jazz. But
19 this week ... he started singing! In class! Out loud! So we
20 could all hear him! Who does that? Especially teachers!
21 They're usually reserved and stiff, and let's be honest, not
22 a whole lot of fun. But this guy — Mr. Wright — he's
23 practically dancing around the room, singing this song
24 about the war. And get this! He wants *us* to sing along too!
25 In fact, he's throwing out bonus points to anyone that will
26 sing with him! It's like singing karaoke in class. I've heard

1   of other teachers playing music in class. But singing along?
2   In social studies? I knew they called him the "rock star" of
3   the school. Now I know why.

5. My Teenage Father

(Girl or Guy)

1   There are reasons why parents should never get
2 divorced. And not just the obvious ones, either. Let me tell
3 you from firsthand experience that having parents who are
4 dating is far worse than parents who are fighting. I would
5 much rather go back to the days when my parents were
6 screaming at each other at the top of their lungs — so
7 loudly, in fact, that I could still hear them over my sound-
8 blocking headphones with my music at the highest level
9 possible. But even that is better than what I have to hear
10 now. *All the time.*
11   It's my dad. He's got this new girlfriend, and he's acting
12 like a love-struck teenager. When he's not whispering stuff
13 to her over the phone, he's giggling like a schoolgirl over a
14 text she's sent him. I didn't even know my dad knew how to
15 text, and now that's all he does. His phone is never out of
16 his hand. Even during dinner, which was always a strict rule
17 when he was married to my mom. *None* of us was allowed
18 to have a phone at the dinner table! Now I bet my dad sends
19 a thousand texts a day! It's a good thing we have an
20 unlimited plan. And when they're not texting, they're calling.
21 And if that's not enough, they're together all the time!
22   But even that's not the worst part! Get this. The other
23 day I actually saw him doodling her name while he was
24 flirting with her on the phone! What respectable guy doodles
25 in the first place? But what forty-five-year-old man does?!
26 It's ludicrous! There were hearts and flowers and everything.
27 I think he's gone completely crazy. Does he not see how
28 childish and overdramatic he's being? He barely even knows

1   her! So take my advice, if your parents tell you they're
2   getting divorced, do everything you can to keep them
3   together! You do *not*, I repeat, *you do not* want to live
4   through something like this! It's enough to make you puke.

6. The End of the World Is Not Coming

(Girl or Guy)

1   So ... did you know the end of the world is right around
2 the corner? That one day when you least expect it — wham,
3 bam, boom! There goes the world! Did you know that? *No!*
4 Of course you didn't! Because *no one* knows when the end
5 of the world is coming ... or *if* the end of the world is *ever*
6 coming! But my parents think they do. They think that we
7 have to believe all that gloom-and-doom stuff and walk
8 around with this ridiculous mentality that every day could be
9 our last. They truly believe that it's going to happen any day
10 now. They're practically in a frenzy over it. Like when a store
11 has an epic sale and people are pushing and shoving to buy
12 the sale items — that's how crazy my parents are acting!
13   They've been hoarding food and water for months now.
14 You should see our basement. It's stocked to the gills! Do
15 you know how many jars of homemade salsa we have down
16 there? I ask you this: is salsa even necessary? I mean, like
17 really, if the end of the world comes, are we going to be
18 munching on tortilla chips and salsa? Maybe we should be
19 hoarding chocolate chip cookies too, because I definitely
20 don't want to run out of those!
21   We've got bottled water, jars of spaghetti sauce — I
22 don't even like spaghetti now, much less if the world has
23 ended! — canned vegetables, boxes of cereal and crackers,
24 and noodles. And countless flashlights and batteries. Not to
25 mention about fifteen rolls of duct tape. Apparently that's
26 the answer to everything when the apocalypse hits — duct
27 tape.

1   You know, they've spent so much time and energy
2 preparing for the end of the world that I think they're
3 actually going to be disappointed if it doesn't end soon. But
4 in the meantime, if anyone needs a jar of salsa, I've got your
5 back.

7. Sleepovers Do Not Require a Fire Drill

(Girl)

1   Do you have fire drills at your house? Like full-fledged
2   "have-to-leave-the-house-in-whatever-it-is-you're -wearing"
3   kind of fire drills? "At-all-hours-of-the-day-or-night" kind of
4   fire drills? No? I didn't think so. Because your family is
5   normal. Or more importantly, your father is probably
6   normal. Mine is not.
7   I know he's a firefighter and all, and I know he's seen
8   some pretty awful things in his life, but come on! There's a
9   thing called *paranoia*. And being obsessed. And there's a
10   time and place for everything, and the middle of my birthday
11   slumber party is *not* the time and place!
12   You should have seen my friends' faces when my dad
13   sounded the fire alarm and then made us shimmy down a
14   sheet that he made into a rope. One girl cried, even though
15   I kept telling her there really wasn't a fire, that it was just
16   my crazy dad. I don't think she'll ever spend the night here
17   again. Who could blame her? She was woken up from a
18   dead sleep to a man yelling at her with a megaphone to stay
19   low and then climb out a two-story window on a sheet!
20   It may sound like fun, but believe me, it's not! It's totally
21   annoying and embarrassing. Besides, with all the alarms in
22   my house, I'm pretty sure that at the first whiff of smoke,
23   I'll be jerked out of the house so fast, I will never have the
24   chance to get trapped in my bedroom and have to climb
25   down a sheet!
26   And it's not just at the house that he acts this way.
27   Every time we go somewhere, my dad drills us on where the

1   fire exits are located and what our plan of action would be
2   in the case of an emergency. I know he only does it because
3   he loves us, but man, I just want to go somewhere one time
4   and *not* have to worry about where they keep their fire
5   extinguisher!

8. I Don't Want to Live in Kansas Anymore, Toto

(Girl or Guy)

1   I never thought it would happen in my town. We'd never
2 even come close to having one before, and then this past
3 spring we had not only one ... but two tornadoes! One
4 ripped right through my neighborhood, and I can tell you
5 that it was the scariest thing I've ever lived through! The
6 whole house shook and the sky was so dark in the middle
7 of the day that it looked like midnight outside. It was weird
8 because just earlier my sister and I had been lying out on
9 the back porch trying to work on our tans and it was a
10 gorgeous day out. The storm came out of nowhere.
11   I thought my mom was being extra cautious when she
12 made us go to the basement. But I guess I should've known
13 better because my mom *never* makes us go down there.
14 Usually we sit out on the front porch and watch storms go
15 by. But this one was eerie right from the start. And then
16 when it got so dark and we heard this really loud thunderous
17 noise, I knew we were in trouble. I promise that I have never
18 been that scared in my life. I kind of always thought it would
19 be fun to experience something like that — you know, to say
20 you survived the Great Tornado of Williamsburg. But I never
21 ever will think that again! I've had nightmares about it for
22 months. The whole top half of our house was ripped off! We
23 found some of our stuff miles away in a field! There is
24 nothing exciting or fun about that.
25   I think my mom — who used to love storms — has
26 almost convinced my dad to move. Far, far north. Like

1   Alaska or somewhere where things like this don't happen. I
2   am all for it! I don't know why Dorothy wanted to go home
3   to Kansas so badly. I say, get me out of here!

9. My Own Kind of Makeup

(Girl)

1   It's *my* face. I don't understand why I can't do what I
2 want to with it. I don't tell *her* what to wear or how to look
3 or what color to dye her hair. Although if I did, I would
4 definitely tell her that those black roots went out years ago!
5 It's just not fair that just because she's the mother, she
6 gets to tell me what to do about *my* body. And she's not
7 even my *real* mother anyway. She's my dad's wife. My
8 stepmother. She shouldn't be making rules for me anyway.
9 I know if Dad had half a clue about how horrible she's being,
10 he would take my side! But he's so clueless. He thinks that
11 just because she's a woman, that she should make all the
12 girl-related decisions about me! Well, just because *she* likes
13 to be plain old Jane with no makeup doesn't mean that I
14 want to be. What self-respecting girl would?
15   Besides, *her* skin is smooth and flawless. Probably
16 because she's too old for zits! But *mine* is blotchy and
17 spotty. I *need* makeup. So can you blame me that I've taken
18 matters into my own hands? I have to be sneaky though
19 since she checks my purse. Yeah, that's right. She actually
20 looks through my *personal* belongings to make sure I'm not
21 sneaking makeup to school. But you know what I figured
22 out? Black marker makes great eyeliner. And the slightly
23 tinted red lip balm that you use on chapped lips ... well, it
24 can be used on your cheeks as blush.
25   The hardest thing to figure out was what to use for
26 foundation, which I need more than ever. But a little trial
27 and error and a whole lot of persistence finally paid off! I
28 figured out that hand lotion with a little soy sauce added in

1   made just the right color! It smells a little at first before it
2   dries on my face, but who gets that close to my face
3   anyway? And we eat Chinese so much I have tons of those
4   little packets of sauce! So plain Jane might *think* she's won
5   this round, but she hasn't! She can't outsmart me!

10. I Look Like a Boy!

(Girl)

1 "Oops!"

2 That's what I heard my sister say at a time I definitely
3 did *not* want to hear such an exclamation! She was wielding
4 scissors at the back of my head, performing what was
5 supposed to be a simple trim.

6 "Don't worry, I can fix it," she said, and though she tried
7 to sound calm, I could hear a little panic in her voice. It
8 made the hairs on the back of my neck stand up. But I
9 didn't stop her. I figured, how bad could it be? She wasn't
10 adding layers or anything sophisticated, just taking an inch
11 or so off the bottom.

12 "Hmmmm," she said, as she made her way around to
13 my face. "Maybe if I just trimmed up the bangs a little too."
14 She chewed her lip as she concentrated on cutting my
15 bangs, and I should've known by the fact that her lower lip
16 was no longer pink but white that things were not going
17 well. But still, I didn't panic. I wasn't overly vain or majorly
18 into hairstyles. A simple straight cut was easy to style and
19 all that I ever wanted.

20 "Let me just even this out." Her eyes darted back and
21 forth. "Don't worry; I've got it all under control."

22 Under control? That didn't sound too good. "Under
23 control" is what you say when talking about a wildfire. Or a
24 mob of people. Or even some rowdy kids. It definitely was
25 not what you said when trimming up hair that was straight
26 as a pin and definitely already "under control."

27 And that's when I looked. And looked. And looked. And
28 then right after that is when I cried. And cried. And cried.

1 My so-called beauty school sister had turned me into a boy!
2 To make things worse, the next day when I was walking
3 home from school I heard two little kids say, "Look at the
4 boy with earrings!"
5 Never again would I volunteer to be her hair dummy!

11. Slumber Party Terror

(Girl)

1 I knew I shouldn't have agreed to stay at Sarah's house
2 the other night. One, I don't really like her. And two,
3 sleepovers are just not my thing. The girls always end up
4 doing stupid silly things like truth or dare or dance parties
5 or, even worse, karaoke. So I guess I could be thankful that
6 none of that happened that night. But now I wish it had,
7 because ever since that night, I have to sleep with a light
8 on. I can't sleep in the dark. And I've always loved the dark.

9 It isn't hard to remember exactly everything that
10 happened because I can't stop the mental tape from playing
11 over and over in my head. I was sitting on the couch beside
12 prissy Morgan Beechmont when the banging first started. I
13 remember how she jumped and clutched the edge of the
14 couch. "What is that?" she yelled. But before we could even
15 investigate, the sliding door was pushed open and two men
16 in ski masks came running into the room.

17 I'm proud to say that my first instinct was to run and
18 hide. I darted down the hall and hid in the bathroom closet
19 — underneath a pile of dirty smelly clothes. I could hear
20 screams from the living room and I pictured horrible things
21 happening in there. Then I could hear laughter.

22 That confused me. Were the masked men so sick that
23 they were laughing about what they'd done? But as I
24 listened longer, I was positive that it was the girls laughing.
25 Even still, I stayed huddled down. Even when I heard
26 banging around the house and people shouting my name.
27 Finally I felt a hand on my shoulder. I screamed. I couldn't
28 help it.

1   "You can come out now," Sarah's mom said, softly. "It
2   was all just a horrible joke."
3   That got me out of the closet fast. A joke? Someone
4   really thought that was funny? I guess you could see the
5   anger on my face. My mom says I'm like an open book when
6   it comes to my emotions. I'm sure they could tell that I
7   didn't think it was funny at all. That's when things went
8   from bad to unbelievably bad. Sarah's father, who was one
9   of the men in the ski masks by the way, brought all the girls
10   back into the living room and used me as an example of
11   what you should do if an intruder enters your house! Like
12   this was a life lesson we should learn from! I called my mom
13   that instant and went home. Next time, if I agree to sleep
14   over at someone's house ever again, I will be more than
15   happy to play truth or dare!

12. Was That Supposed to Be a Kiss?

(Girl)

1　I always knew my first kiss would be memorable,
2　because I was determined to wait for the perfect boy. Even
3　if that meant I was in college before it ever happened. That's
4　why I kind of feel robbed that I had my first kiss when I
5　didn't even want it. In fact, I'm not even sure if it counts, or
6　I guess, if I have to count it. Are there rules on this kind of
7　thing? Like just because a boy shoved his face onto mine,
8　do I have to say it was my first kiss?
9　I was just walking around the corner from the back
10　hallway at the swim meet, replaying the heat I had just
11　swum. If only I had pushed a little harder, I could've gotten
12　second place instead of third. Maybe even first. So it was
13　completely unexpected when Bo Thomas appeared suddenly
14　in front of my face. Like really close.
15　"You swam great," he said, and then he was thrusting
16　his face toward mine. I guess I was too shocked to even
17　move because the next thing I know, his tongue was up my
18　nose! That's right! Up my nose! And then he was gone. I'm
19　really not sure that this even counts because one, I don't
20　think his lips came anywhere close to mine, and two, his
21　tongue was *up my nose!* That's just gross! How could he
22　even miss like that? And why was his tongue out in the first
23　place?
24　I knew I always wanted my first kiss to be memorable,
25　but I didn't mean like this! Though I can certainly say I will
26　*never* forget it.

13. Rollerblading Rocks

(Guy)

1   I know it's not the manliest thing in the world, but I
2 really don't care what anyone thinks. I have fun, it's good
3 exercise, and it's something I can do with my brother and
4 dad. So who cares if everyone else thinks that rollerblading
5 was a thing of the eighties? Why is it cooler to be on roller
6 skates or a skateboard? I mean, is there really a difference
7 when you're talking about the "cool" factor if the wheels are
8 somehow under your feet? The only wheels that could ever
9 make you look cool might be if you were sitting on a Harley.
10 Or maybe a pickup truck or an awesome Jeep to go four-
11 wheeling in.

12   So it really isn't about being cool. Obviously. It's more
13 about the time I get to spend with my dad. He only gets one
14 day off a week from driving his rig, so it's pretty awesome
15 that he spends it at the park with my brother and me. It
16 kind of stinks that we've only had one day a week with him
17 our whole lives, but honestly it's more than a lot of my
18 friends get with their parents who are home all the time.
19 Because when Dad's home, he's home. He doesn't do
20 anything but spend time with us. He barely sleeps! When
21 Dad's home, we rollerblade, watch movies, eat pizza, play
22 cards. Every Sunday is almost like a holiday or a snow day.

23   That's why I don't care what my friends say about me
24 rollerblading. They're just jealous because their dads would
25 rather watch sports or read boring articles about the stock
26 market or go to the gym and work out. My dad is cool, and
27 I'd play hopscotch if that's what he wanted to do!

14. Banned from Television

(Guy)

1　There's something seriously wrong with me. Every time
2　I think I know what I want to do with my life, I watch a movie
3　or television show and it makes me change my mind. It's
4　gotten really ridiculous. The other night I was watching a
5　cooking show, and for at least two days, I wanted to be a
6　chef. In the past year, I've wanted to be a forensic crime
7　scene investigator, a fireman, a body builder, a famous
8　singer, guitar player, lawyer ... and the list goes on.
9　And I don't mean just a fleeting thought. I mean I
10　seriously think for an hour, a day, a month — however long
11　until I see another show that convinces me otherwise — that
12　I really want to be those things. Like desperately deep down
13　in my soul. Like I'll *die* if I can't be them. I even research
14　the options on the Internet and look up the average pay. But
15　not even the jobs with crummy salaries change my mind
16　once I've made it up. Well, not until the next show changes
17　my mind again.
18　The worst was on Saturday morning when my baby
19　brother was watching some kiddie cartoon about a train,
20　and all of a sudden I wanted to be a train conductor! Do
21　they even have those anymore? And why would a cartoon be
22　able to influence my life? It's a cartoon, for crying out loud!
23　So I'm thinking that I need to ban myself from
24　television. Can you believe that? A kid my age *not* watching
25　TV? How weird would that be? But how else am I going to
26　figure out what I *really* want to be? Because if I'm not
27　careful, I may end up wanting to be a ballerina or runway
28　model!

15. Lefties Are Righties

(Girl or Guy)

1   My teacher has lost her mind! Not your normal crazy
2   kind of lost your mind, but bona fide "needs to be
3   committed" kind of lost her mind! You know what she's
4   trying to do? Let me tell you! She's trying to create her own
5   little army of what she calls "perfect students," that's what!
6   And you want to know what she just did? Of course you do!
7   She forced all of us "lefties" in the room to write with our
8   right hands. Said she wouldn't tolerate left-handed
9   nonsense anymore. That clearly right-handed people are
10 smarter, more creative, more responsible, behave better in
11 class, and on and on. She had a whole list of reasons why
12 right-handed people are better than left-handed people! It's
13 completely insulting!
14   Well, that's complete bull! You just wait 'til my left-
15 handed father finds out! My successful stock broker, six-
16 figure-salary father! Yeah, that's right. Left-handed people
17 are *not* stupider ... I mean, more stupid. Left-handed people
18 rock. In fact, I'd say that left-handed people are *better* than
19 right-handed people. Like my dad. None of my friends'
20 fathers are as successful as he is. So maybe you've got it
21 all wrong, Mrs. Atkins. Maybe all right-handed people
22 should be forced to write with their left hands! Or go to a
23 different school ... or live in a different place ... (Pause)
24   What? Oh ... well, this is embarrassing ... I didn't realize
25 you were making a point about ... Of course I knew you
26 didn't really mean it. I was just joking, of course. Clearly
27 there is no difference between right-handed people and left-
28 handed people ... well, other than the obvious.
29   Sorry, Mrs. Atkins. I'll sit down now.

16. A Watched Clock Never Boils

(Girl or Guy)

1   So my grandmother always says funny things like, "A
2 watched clock never boils" instead of a "watched pot." And
3 then she gets upset when I don't understand her! But how
4 am I supposed to make heads or tails out of half the things
5 she says? Just the other day I asked her which way was
6 faster to get to my house from school, and she said, "It's
7 half a dozen." That was it. Like it made sense. A half dozen
8 of what? So I looked up old sayings online, and it's
9 supposed to be, "Six one way or half a dozen the other."
10 Which makes sense, right? Because it's basically saying it's
11 the same either way. Why couldn't she just say that? I
12 swear it's like breaking a code every time I talk to her!

13   One of my favorites was when she said, "Don't throw
14 out the bath water, just the baby!" I was like, *What?!* Who
15 throws out babies? Then I found out that it's, "Don't throw
16 the baby out with the bath water." I still don't understand
17 what that means, but it sounds a whole lot better than
18 throwing out babies.

19   Sometimes I think life would be a whole lot easier without
20 her and her funny sayings, but you know what they say,
21 "Don't cut off your nose and spit in your face." No ... wait ...
22 "Don't cut off your face." No, that's not right either ...

23   Wait! I got it! "Don't cut off your nose to spite your
24 face!" Which means if I want my grandma around, I have to
25 put up with her face! Ha, ha, ha!

17. It's Eighty Degrees, and I'm Shivering

(Girl or Guy)

1   Can you hear that? It's my teeth chattering! For real. I
2   am so cold my teeth are rattling and my fingers and toes are
3   purple! You'd think it was the middle of winter and I lived in
4   Alaska or something. But no! Here I am in sunny eighty-
5   degree weather in South Georgia, and I'm freezing like a
6   Popsicle.

7   Why do places crank the air conditioning so low that it
8   becomes arctic? Don't we wait all winter long to get warm,
9   and then we finally get some great weather, and bam! It's
10   like winter on the inside now!

11   Aren't we supposed to be more energy-conscious than
12   this? Save the earth and all that? Is it really very "green" to
13   keep it fifty degrees in here? Why would any restaurant
14   think it's pleasant to eat in a place this cold? Of course the
15   chattering of my teeth means less chewing, right?

16   I think I am going to boycott eating out until winter when
17   I can actually be warm again! At least then they'll have the
18   heat on!

18. The Round House

(Girl or Guy)

1   "Are you an alien?" "Is that a spaceship?" "What planet
2 are you from?" Yeah, yeah. I've heard it all before. Everyone
3 thinks they are so original, so clever — but believe me, there
4 isn't anything I haven't heard at least a thousand times.
5 Everyone's a comedian, that's for sure.
6   What were my parents thinking when they built this
7 house? No respectable person builds a house that's round,
8 made of metal, and has a string of lights around the roof!
9 Thanks, Dad, for leaving our Christmas lights up year round.
10 Could they really not think that through a little?
11   I have actually had kids in the neighborhood scratch me
12 to see if I bleed red and not some kind of colored alien goo.
13 So can you really blame me that after a while I decided to
14 embrace the idea? Right down to making up my own
15 language and personal alien look? I mean really, who could
16 resist an opportunity like that? Can I help it that the little
17 neighbor kids are terrified now and that they won't play
18 outside in their yards? Or that people walk their dogs on the
19 other side of the street? I know the parents just think I'm a
20 freak, but the kids ... well, it's just soooo easy. Even a
21 simple flashlight can wreak havoc.
22   So when the neighbors run us out of the neighborhood,
23 my parents only have themselves to blame. Maybe next time
24 they'll build a standard square house.
25   But you know ... come to think of it ... where's the fun
26 in that?

19. Wish Obsessed

(Girl or Guy)

1   I don't know who came up with all the wish rules, but
2 they must've been crazy! Like you can't tell someone what
3 you wish for. Who can *not* do that? And why should it
4 matter? A wish shouldn't have restrictions. Or what about
5 the "you have to blow out all the candles to get your wish"
6 rule? I've got asthma! I can't blow that hard. So I'm
7 supposed to be penalized a whole wish because my lungs
8 aren't as strong as the next guy's? That's not even fair.
9   The worst one is the make-a-wish-on-the-time rule. You
10 know the one. You make a wish at eleven-eleven or two-
11 twenty-two or three-thirty-three. Whenever the numbers are
12 all the same. All I can do now is watch the clock! I don't
13 want to let a wish opportunity pass me by. I've got a whole
14 list of stuff I need to wish for.
15   I know it's silly, but what if it's not? What if there really
16 is some kind of wish karma and I let those wishing
17 moments go by? It would be like throwing a winning lottery
18 ticket out the window!
19   My mom says I need to stop. She's even threatened
20 grounding me if I don't stop wishing so much! Can she even
21 do that? What kind of person stops someone from wishing?
22 But she says I'm hurting myself by being so obsessed ...
23 just because I almost passed out from holding my breath in
24 a really loooong tunnel. What's the big deal? And just
25 because I stayed up *all* night watching for a shooting star!
26   Well, I know what I'm wishing for in five minutes when
27 the clock hits four-forty-four! For my mother to get off my
28 back ... Oh crud! I wasn't supposed to tell you that. These
29 darn wish rules are making me crazy!

20. Remote Review

(Girl or Guy)

1   OK, Mom. Now listen up. I'm only going to go over this
2 *one more time.* See this remote? This long skinny black
3 remote that says Panasonic? That's the television remote.
4 You use it to turn the television off and on. You can also
5 adjust the volume with this remote and change the channel.
6 See how it is clearly marked for that? You also use this *same*
7 remote to change the input. What is input, you ask? Well,
8 I've made a quick reference note card for you. See how I've
9 even color-coded what button you need to push? You just
10 need to refer to this when you want to watch a DVD or play
11 your Wii zumba game. Or even if you want to surf the
12 Internet. Remember how our television can go to Facebook,
13 YouTube, and other cool places?
14   Now this small remote — it's for the sound bar. This is
15 where — yep, you guessed it — you get the added sound
16 from. You want to use this when you watch movies or when
17 you do your video weight loss program so that you can turn
18 the sound up really loud. This one is really easy. See this
19 button? That's all you have to do. You press the power
20 button and it will do the rest. You just basically use the up
21 and down volume buttons. Or if you're feeling really
22 adventurous, you can even press the mute button when
23 Grandma calls so that you don't have any sound and you
24 can talk on your phone.
25   OK, moving on. This remote is for the DVD player. You
26 only need to use this one when — yep, you got it again —
27 you want to watch a movie. This remote lets you start and
28 stop the movie or skip to other parts of the DVD.

1   OK, now for the last one. The most tricky of all. This is
2 the remote that gets you to all the shows you've set up to
3 tape. Don't let it scare you. I know it has a *lot* of buttons.
4 But you really only need to use a few. I've put little white
5 dots on the important ones. You can ignore the rest.
6   Oh, wait, there's one more. This one is for the VCR, but
7 really, Mom. That's so eighties, you just need to get rid of
8 it. Yeah, I know you love those old movies, but trust me, you
9 can get anything on DVD now, and the quality is *so* much
10 better.
11   So ... you're all set, right? I can go back upstairs, right?
12 Because I don't want to just get up there and then hear you
13 hollering again.
14   That's right ... you can do it ... no, Mom, it's the other
15 one ... OK ... I'm leaving now ...

21. White as a Ghost

(Girl or Guy)

1 My mother is a maniac. A complete and utter lunatic. I
2 understand why, of course. I'm not completely stupid. But
3 one little mole scare, and now my whole family is on
4 lockdown from the sun! It's like living in a cave! She won't
5 let me open my blinds anymore or even think about pulling
6 back my curtains. And she changed all the curtains to those
7 heavy room-darkening ones that make it pitch black in here!
8 Not an ounce of sunlight can find its way into our house!
9   And if that's not bad enough, she makes us lather up
10 with sunscreen every time we walk out the door. Does she
11 really think I'm in danger of sunburn at seven a.m.? She's
12 got a whole basket of sun care products by the front and
13 back doors. Every SPF you can think of. We've got sprays,
14 lotions, face creams, and lip balms. The funny thing is ...
15 there isn't even a spot of skin hardly left for the sun to even
16 hit! She's got us covering up from head to toe. Long pants,
17 long sleeves, bandanas on our heads. *(Mimicking mother)*
18 "You have to worry about your scalp, you know! It's a very
19 tender spot that most people forget about!" Yeah. Most
20 *normal* people forget about it.
21   But you know what the most absolute crazy part about
22 all this is? She wants to move our family to Seattle! In
23 Washington! Like all the way across the country! Just
24 because the sun hardly ever shines there. Gee, Mom. Can
25 you sell that idea a little more? Because who the heck wants
26 to live in a place like that?

22. Gurgling Gut

(Girl or Guy)

1 This is *so* embarrassing! Can you hear that? I think I am
2 going to have to stop eating altogether. A stomach is *not*
3 supposed to make this much noise! It's like a construction
4 site going on in there. And what can I do about it? Nothing!
5 It's not like I'm trying to gurgle like a bubbling pot of soup!
6 But everyone looks at me like one, I'm doing it on purpose,
7 and two, I'm the most disgusting person they've ever seen!
8   I've tried keeping a journal of what I eat to see if some
9 things are worse than others, but no! Everything is the
10 same. What am I supposed to do with that? A person has
11 to eat. I even tried a total liquid diet for a few days, and you
12 guessed it, it was worse! Well, why wouldn't it be, right? All
13 that liquid sloshing around in here? And to top things off, I
14 was starving to death!
15   The only option left is to only be in loud places, which
16 honestly isn't as hard as it sounds. Even in school, most of
17 my classes are pretty rowdy. One benefit of not being in
18 advanced classes, I might add. The only time it gets really
19 quiet is test time, so I've come up with a game plan. I'll just
20 be sick those days and take my make-up tests after school
21 when no one but the teacher is around. Still embarrassing,
22 but not near as bad as the whole class hearing this ruckus
23 in my stomach.
24   The only problem left is Mr. Doyal's class. You literally
25 can hear a pin drop in there! I think he was in the army or
26 something, because he runs his class like being in the
27 service. He even uses military time. Problem is ... I actually
28 love his class! Not only is it a history class, he's actually a

1 really cool teacher, even though he's more strict than most.
2 He makes it fun ... in a really structured way, of course!
3 But I guess there's really no way around it, with a
4 classroom that quiet ... I'm going to have to get my
5 schedule switched! Even though the only option left is
6 geometry! Argh!

23. Uncle Dad

(Girl or Guy)

1   Is it weird that I think my mom's boyfriend is better than
2 my real dad? I guess that's not very loyal of me, huh? But
3 can you really blame me? My dad kind of checked out on us
4 years ago. Oh, he's around physically ... if you count living
5 in the same town. But emotionally, he hasn't really
6 connected to me in years.

7   I can't even remember the last "real" conversation we
8 had. All we talk about now is the weather or what we're
9 going to eat when he picks me up for dinner on those rare
10 occasions when he actually does pick me up to go
11 somewhere and doesn't bail at the last moment. I swear my
12 dad has more work emergencies than anyone I know. And
13 he's an accountant! Is there really such a thing as a work
14 emergency when you're a number cruncher?

15   It's so weird having awkward conversations with the
16 man who's known me since birth. Sometimes he feels more
17 like a distant uncle or cousin instead of my dad. You know,
18 the kind of relative you only see once or twice a year if that.

19   I guess I could be happy that he's not all up in my
20 business, but it'd be nice to know that he actually cares
21 enough to find out what's going on in my life. Mom says he's
22 never been much of a talker. That he just doesn't know how
23 to express himself. Well, he sure knew how to express
24 himself at dinner the other night. He talked about the bread
25 for ten minutes straight! The bread! I don't even think a
26 baker can talk about bread for that long!

27   Oh well. I guess I'll take what I can get with good old
28 Uncle Dad.

24. My Brother Thinks He's a Cowboy

(Girl or Guy)

1   The worst thing my parents ever did was buy my brother
2 Thomas a cowboy hat for his birthday. The kid thinks he's
3 a cowboy now! Like for real. I'm not kidding. He "draws" his
4 gun — fake finger gun only, of course; my parents aren't
5 *that* crazy — every time I turn around. And he rides his fake
6 horse everywhere!
7   It was bad enough when it was just around the house.
8 Now he's doing it out in public, and my parents are acting
9 oblivious to it all! He looks completely ridiculous. Isn't he a
10 little too old to be pretending like that? He's eight years old,
11 galloping around on a fake horse with a fake gun and
12 fighting off fake train robbers, bank robbers, horse thieves,
13 or aliens. Yeah, that's right. Aliens. Apparently that's the
14 job of cowboys now. Protecting the earth from
15 extraterrestrials.
16   The worst is his fake cowboy drawl and the piece of
17 grass he keeps hanging out of his mouth. That's just plain
18 disgusting! Does he know what germs are on that grass? We
19 have a dog, for Pete's sake. When I was little, my mom
20 wouldn't even let me eat a cookie that hit the kitchen floor,
21 and now Thomas is putting pee-soaked grass in his mouth,
22 and that's OK?
23   Mom keeps telling me it's just a phase and that it will
24 pass soon. All I know is that if Thomas points his fake gun
25 in my face one more time, I'm going to break his little
26 cowboy finger!

25. If I Were the President

(Girl or Guy)

1   If I were the President, I would make it a law that every
2   kid in America had to have a dog. Or I guess if they prefer,
3   a cat.

4   If I were the President, I would make it a law that kids
5   only had to go to school on rainy days in the spring, because
6   who wants to waste a pretty sunny spring day inside? And
7   there's nothing to do on those dreary days anyway.

8   If I were the President, I would make it a law that video
9   games are just as educational as books so that parents
10 wouldn't limit the time we're allowed to play them.

11 If I were the President, I would make it a law that all
12 parents have to drive their kids to and from school because
13 riding on the bus is like the most awful part of every day. *No*
14 *one* likes to ride on the bus.

15 If I were the President, I would make it a law that every
16 day was pizza day at school, because who likes those nasty
17 rubbery fried chunks of meat that they try to pass off as
18 chicken nuggets? And absolutely *no one* likes those mystery
19 meat and gravy days!

20 If I were the President, I would make it a law that
21 everyone should get a million dollars because it's just not
22 fair that some people are rich and some people are poor. My
23 dad says that makes me a Democrat, but I think it just
24 makes me nice and considerate, because who the heck
25 doesn't want to be rich?

26 So that's what I'd do if I were the President.

26. Memory Math

(Girl or Guy)

1   I have a great memory. I can name every state in
2 alphabetical order — frontwards and backwards. And I can
3 tell you the capitol of each one. I can rattle off all the major
4 wars and tell you who was involved and what year they
5 occurred. I can tell you the batting averages of the top ten
6 baseball players in America. I can even tell you all the
7 abbreviations in the periodic table.

8   So why can't I memorize the multiplication tables? We
9 were supposed to have those down by fourth grade, and
10 here I am in middle school now, and I still can't get them
11 right consistently. It's like my mind goes completely blank
12 when it comes to math. I think part of it is because of *how*
13 we had to learn them. Mrs. Crabapple — I swear that's
14 really her name — made us stand up in front of class and
15 recite them to the beat she banged out on a set of bongo
16 drums. I am dead serious! Do you have any idea how nerve-
17 wracking that was? Everyone staring at you, laughing if you
18 missed a beat. If you were doing well, she just beat the
19 drums faster to try and mess you up. I think it was her own
20 private way of jerking us around. I'm sure she laughed
21 about it with her friends — if she even had any — at night.

22   She's scarred me for life, I think. Now whenever I need
23 to do multiplication in my head, all I hear is a beating drum!
24 How am I ever going to be an engineer if I can't do math?

25   Thanks, Mrs. Crabapple. You've ruined my future career!
26 I will probably never even make it to college now!

27. I'd Rather Die Than Give a Speech ... What?

(Girl or Guy)

1   Did you know that more people are afraid of public
2 speaking than they are afraid of dying? Of dying! Isn't that
3 crazy? What's the worst thing that can possibly happen to
4 you when you're giving a speech? But think of all the
5 horrible, terrible, gross, and scary ways there are to die!

6   Really, what can happen? You forget what you're saying?
7 Or you stumble over your words? Or maybe you even trip
8 on-stage? Or let's even say the worst happens and you let
9 a bodily noise slip out when everyone is quiet. But even if
10 *that* were to happen, is any of that really *more* scary than
11 dying? That is so out of whack!

12   I love giving speeches and presentations, anything
13 where I get to be front and center. What's more thrilling
14 than having everyone's eyes on you? Watching your every
15 move. Hanging on your every word. It's exhilarating. Like
16 being famous for a few moments. I wish all my classes made
17 us give presentations! It's like an easy A for me. Everyone
18 says I'm a natural at it. Some even say I should be a
19 newscaster or maybe even a comedian. Wouldn't that be
20 awesome to be paid for basically just talking? I wouldn't
21 even have to break a sweat.

22   I sure don't get being less afraid of dying! I think
23 someone misunderstood. Surely no one really thinks public
24 speaking is *that* bad. I say, bring it on!

28. Zitty Zellerman

(Girl)

1   OK, I know this is mean, and I probably shouldn't even
2   say it out loud because it's so mean and you're probably
3   going to judge me for it ... but I just can't stop staring at
4   this boy in my class. Not because he's cute ... believe me,
5   it's definitely *not* that at all! It's because his face is covered
6   in zits! Like all over! Zitty Zellerman is what I call him in my
7   head. I would never say it out loud, though, because that's
8   just awful, and I'm really not an awful person! I feel bad
9   even thinking it. But how can I help it? I've never seen so
10   many zits in my life. Not on one face. It's like a game now.
11   I can't even help it. I sit and stare and play connect the
12   dots. Or try and count them — impossible, I might add —
13   or look for constellations or geometric designs. The
14   possibilities are endless.
15   I feel bad for the poor guy. It's not that I don't. It would
16   be awful to have all that going on with your face. And he's
17   a really nice guy, which makes me feel even worse. But I
18   swear it's like a train wreck. I can't take my eyes off it! I try.
19   I really, really do.
20   And now this is going to sound the meanest of all, but I
21   really hope the poor guy gets something to clear that up
22   soon, because my grades are starting to slip in here. I'm
23   afraid if he keeps distracting me, I'm going to fail! Maybe I
24   should try changing seats!

29. That Is Not a Vacation Spot

(Girl or Guy)

1   I know every kid says this, and it probably isn't really
2   even true, but in this case you have to believe me that my
3   father is the absolute weirdest man ever. I love him to
4   pieces, but he is the epitome of geek. Or nerd. Or freak.
5   Take your pick. I wouldn't even care if it only affected him.
6   But his quirkiness is affecting the whole family. I just want
7   to be normal. Do normal things. Take *normal* family
8   vacations. Like my friend Sara. They go to Myrtle Beach
9   every year. Same time, same place. Maybe a little boring if
10   you ask me, but *normal* all the same. Or my friend Jack. His
11   family is all about exotic vacations. They've been to Greece,
12   the Netherlands, even to Fiji. Yeah, *Fiji*. Who takes their
13   kids to *Fiji*?
14   Want to know where my father takes us? Wait. Let me
15   see if you can guess. Have you ever heard of the famous
16   courthouse with the tree in it? *Of course you haven't!* Who
17   the heck has? It's in Greensburg, Indiana. Sounds like a fun
18   place, huh? Where the main attraction is foliage growing out
19   of a building? You don't want to miss excitement like that.
20   I swear he finds the most obscure places and then
21   makes them into a family vacation. But let me ask you this,
22   how long can you possibly spend looking up at a tree? Not
23   long, I tell you. Another time we drove a day and a half to
24   see the world's largest baseball bat. I'm not kidding. That
25   was some major excitement for him. And to make things
26   even better, we *got* to tour the factory that actually makes

1   baseball bats. Yeah, I said *got* to, because that's my dad's
2   response to everything. I say, "Do we *have* to?" and he says,
3   "No, you *get* to." Like it's a big deal or something, and I
4   should be eternally grateful for the opportunity to share in
5   something amazing like watching pieces of wood get shaped
6   into ... different pieces of wood.
7   I swear it's made me dread summer vacation. And that's
8   *just not normal!* What kid in the world doesn't count the
9   days until school is out? But geez, I can be bored here just
10 as easily as those stupid places, and at least my friends are
11 at school!

30. Virtual Friend Fanatic

(Girl)

1   I think my sister may need therapy. It's almost as bad
2 as when little kids have invisible friends that they think they
3 see. Like my cousin Allen who had to have a place set at
4 the table for his friend Gary. He did that for years, and
5 everyone just acted like he was part of the family. Well, my
6 sister's friends aren't invisible, they're virtual! She has this
7 whole town set up on her computer, and she talks about
8 them and worries about them and *obsesses* over them like
9 they're real!
10   It's gotten so bad that she doesn't hardly ever leave the
11 house to go see *real* people. She used to have a lot of
12 friends. Now no one ever comes to see her, and she doesn't
13 ever talk on the phone or text anyone. The only thing that
14 matters is her computer and her virtual friends and family.
15 Want to know what happened the other night? We had to
16 bring her dinner home because she wouldn't go out to eat
17 with us! She said she was having problems with one of her
18 sisters and needed to stay on top of things to get it figured
19 out. *One of her sisters?* I am her *only* sister! And she sure
20 doesn't seem too worried about fixing things with me!
21   I can't remember the last time I actually got eye contact
22 from her, much less an actual conversation. A grunt does
23 *not* count as conversation, by the way! I don't know how my
24 parents can stand it. Shouldn't they be worried about this
25 unnatural obsession? It's one thing to be seven and feed a
26 fake person at a tea party, but fifteen and the only friends
27 you have are not even three-dimensional? That's something
28 to worry about! And I'm not just saying that because she
29 replaced me with a computer character!

31. It Is but It Isn't Me

(Girl or Guy)

There's something to be said for anonymity. Although in this case, I guess everyone knows who I am. It's just a whole other thing when I don't have to be face to face. I feel like a completely different person. More confident. More cool. It's not like I'm trying to be someone else ... it just happens automatically.

That's why I love social media. I love posting on people's walls. Making comments on statuses. Writing messages. It's so easy to be clever and witty when you don't have to do it in the blink of an eye. I can think things out. Make a plan of what I want to say.

It's not that I'm trying to be someone I'm not. When I get in front of a computer screen and keyboard, it *is* who I am. I swear a transformation occurs the minute I sit down. I don't even feel self-conscious or insecure like I do when I'm at school. It's just so easy online. I can see why some people get addicted to being online. It's completely awesome.

That's why I love texting too. What's better than having a conversation in short little sentences instead of big long hot-aired paragraphs? It's just so easy to pop quippy little things. Add a smiley face or a frowny face and you're done.

Real-time conversations are so awkward. I can never think of the right thing to say. Not until after the person has walked away. Then I think of all the funny things I should have said instead of babbling on and on about something stupid, like Mr. Henry's math quiz. Who cares about that anyway?

1   I just wish I could be the same way in person. You think
2 we'll ever switch to virtual schools? Because that would
3 totally rock! I'd be the most popular kid in the class!

32. Lunchtime Loser

(Girl or Guy)

1   I don't know who decided it was uncool to bring your
2 lunch to school. Why would eating the nasty cafeteria food
3 be the cool thing to do? Have you ever seen the choices they
4 offer us? I really don't understand why everyone thinks it's
5 hilarious that I bring my lunch instead of buying it. I swear
6 it's crazy that I'm the one everyone in class makes fun of.
7 They call me the "Lunchtime Loser." Just because I bring
8 my lunch instead of buying it.
9   Why don't they pick on Gary? He always eats with his
10 mouth full. Or Jack, who likes to put French fries up his
11 nose. Or even Allison. She puts ketchup on everything.
12 Even dessert. How can they think that I am the weird one?
13 Just because I happen to like the kind of lunches my mother
14 makes me? I actually prefer them to paying for food I would
15 never ever eat. I'm a picky eater. I'll admit it. But nothing
16 about the school lunches really appeals to me.
17   They act like it's because I can't afford to buy my lunch,
18 which is ridiculous. Of course I could buy if I wanted to.
19 Which I don't. I think they are just jealous because my
20 mom's sandwiches are like the ones from the deli. She piles
21 on the meat and adds two kinds of cheese and lots of
22 pickles. And she always packs me a bag of chips and some
23 kind of homemade dessert. Like extra chocolate chip
24 cookies or brownies or big slabs of cake. Why would I ever
25 want to give up all that for a rubbery piece of pizza or a piece
26 of greasy fried chicken?
27   So I guess if they want to call me names like
28 "Lunchtime Loser," they can. They're the losers, not me. I

1 love my mom's lunches, and I'm not going to buy my lunch
2 just so I can fit in. Besides, if it wasn't this, it'd be
3 something else. I guess being the "Lunchtime Loser" is
4 better than being "Bathroom Becky" — just because she
5 leaves class to go to the bathroom a lot!

33. Tofu Troubles

(Girl or Guy)

1   I have never felt so guilty in all my life. I can barely sleep
2 at night because I can't stop thinking of what I've done. Or
3 actually what I really, really want to do again. I feel like after
4 that one bite, I became addicted, and now it's all I can think
5 about. See, my parents are vegan, and all I've ever been
6 allowed to eat is vegan food. Yeah, I'm talking tofu
7 everything. And I've always been OK with it. I guess I
8 actually even like it. At least I *did.*

9   Then I spent the night at my friend Tom's house the
10 other night, and they were grilling hamburgers. They offered
11 me a tofu burger, and I was going to eat it — especially after
12 his mom had gone to the trouble of getting one to grill for
13 me — but their burgers just looked so juicy ... and smelled
14 so delicious.

15   I didn't think it would hurt to just eat one. How bad
16 could that possibly be, right? It's just a burger. People eat
17 them all the time. Look at the McDonald's sign. Something
18 like over ninety-nine billion served. Ninety-nine billion! They
19 can't be that bad if they sell so many of them!

20   So maybe I actually ate two that night. But still. I
21 thought that would be it. That I would never want another
22 one. But that sure didn't happen. I really, really want one
23 now. And I feel so awful about it! Like I've let my parents
24 down or something. I swear I feel just as bad as if I had
25 done something really wrong, like smoked or drank!

26   I know I have to tell them. But how will they ever trust
27 me again? Will they even let me hang out at friends' houses
28 anymore? Probably not Tom's, that's for sure. Even though

1 it wasn't his fault. It was totally my choice. He didn't
2 pressure me at all. But they won't believe that. They'll think
3 he's a bad influence since I've never strayed from the diet
4 like that before. You know what? Maybe it's better if I don't
5 tell them. I don't want them banning me from Tom's ...
6 especially since his dad really knows how to grill great
7 burgers ... and if I ever want another one ... Oh gosh, maybe
8 I need therapy!

34. Squeaker

(Guy)

1 I've always been a pretty popular guy with the girls. Not
2 to sound vain or anything, but I think it's the combination
3 of my white-blond hair and the fact that I'm one of the only
4 guys in class who is actually taller than most of the girls. I
5 guess I was lucky to hit puberty before all my friends,
6 because I am a good foot taller than most of the guys I see.
7 But the advantage of going through things first didn't come
8 without a price, believe me.
9 At first I thought I could hide it — the annoying crackling
10 that was happening with my voice. I found that sometimes
11 when I talked, with no warning at all, my voice would crack
12 and squeak like a little girl's. I mean a really young little
13 girl's. Like an annoying four-year-old sister begging you to
14 play with her. To hide this horrifying change in my body, I
15 basically just stopped speaking. All day long. Not in the
16 halls, not at lunch, not in class. Nowhere. I went from a
17 completely social kid to a loner who sat by himself. But
18 what choice did I have?
19 Then the unthinkable happened. Mandatory
20 presentation in science class worth fifty percent of our
21 grade. Fifty percent! No way could I blow that off. I tried to
22 prepare. I must've sucked down two bottles of water with
23 lemon juice and at least two handfuls of cough drops. I even
24 cleared my throat at least five times before I started to
25 speak. And it seemed to be working at first. Then, midway
26 through my presentation, it happened. My voice cracked
27 and suddenly I was talking two octaves higher than usual.
28 Everyone started laughing. Even the teacher, though she

1 tried to hide it. It was soooo embarrassing!
2   And that, my friends, is how I got the nickname
3 "Squeaker." Not even my ultra-blond hair and almost six-
4 foot height can offset a nickname like that. So beware, my
5 friends — you could be next!

35. Witchy Wart

(Girl)

1   I knew it wouldn't work when I did it. I mean, logically
2   there was no way it could. How could burying my
3   grandmother's dishrag in my backyard — a dishrag I had to
4   sneak out of her house — possibly cure a wart that I have
5   growing on my neck? But that shows you just how
6   desperate I was. How desperate I *am*. I've tried everything
7   else, so why not an old wives' tale?
8   What's even worse is the fact that now I'm wondering if
9   it didn't work because maybe I didn't follow the instructions
10   to the T. Maybe I got the wrong kind of dishrag. Maybe my
11   grandmother found out I took it. Maybe I didn't bury it deep
12   enough. Maybe I was supposed to do it during a full moon
13   or something. Or maybe I was supposed to do some kind of
14   chant or something as I buried it. The possibilities are
15   endless.
16   All I know is it didn't work, and I'm still stuck with this
17   ugly wart on my neck that looks like it belongs on a witch's
18   nose. I hate it! It gets caught on my clothes, my necklaces,
19   and even my hair gets tangled around it sometimes.
20   But I've really tried it all. The Band-Aids with the
21   medicine in it. The wart medicine in the little brown bottle.
22   The freeze spray. Everything! My mom says the only thing
23   left is to have the doctor burn it off. *Burn it off!* Now does
24   that not sound crazy to you? Why would I let them *burn*
25   anything off me? If that doesn't sound like an ancient witch
26   doctor sort of thing, what does?
27   So that's why tonight I'm going back to my grandma's
28   house. There's a full moon, and I've prepared a little

1   ceremony to make the burying of the dishrag more official.
2   All I need now is to steal the dishrag and get it buried so
3   that I can keep my mother from letting them take some kind
4   of blowtorch to my neck!

36. Father Has a Six Pack — Not Cool

(Guy)

1   I love my dad more than anything. I do. He's really pretty
2 cool and acts more like my friend than my dad. So I guess
3 I should feel really guilty about the fact that I don't want to
4 be seen with him around my friends, but he's left me no
5 choice.

6   I don't know why he got it in his head that he needed to
7 work out. He looked perfectly fine to me before. But now
8 he's all cut and buff and literally has six-pack abs. I didn't
9 even think anyone but movie stars could really get those.
10 But he has them. And they look great. And his arm muscles
11 ... well, they're to die for! And if he wasn't my dad, I'd be
12 completely stoked for him. Heck, I'd be admiring him from
13 a distance and thinking, "Man, I wish I looked like *that* guy."
14 Which is really the root of the problem. Do you have any idea
15 how awful it is to have your old man look better than you?
16 Isn't he supposed to be old, fat, and flabby by now? I mean,
17 come on! He's almost fifty! He should be balding or turning
18 gray, and maybe even losing his teeth by now!

19   My friends look at him, and then they look at me and I
20 know what they're thinking. They're thinking that this apple
21 sure fell really far from the tree! I look nothing like him! I'm
22 short, plump, and jiggly. My stomach hasn't been flat since
23 I was in second grade! If then! And it certainly wasn't
24 defined like my dad's. I mean, it's practically too much
25 definition. He looks like a body builder. Somehow I've got to
26 get him to stop. Maybe I could make Grandma's cookie

1 recipe that he used to love so much. Or I could add sugar
2 to his protein drinks without him knowing. I know it sounds
3 awful, but you've got to understand ... the man looks like a
4 sculpted statue! I can't compete with that!

37. Two Peas in a Pod

(Girl)

1   You know it was kind of cute when we were little. All the
2 matching outfits, the same style haircut with the same
3 colored bow stuck on top. I think my parents loved the fact
4 that no one but them could really tell us apart. It was
5 almost like a game to them. They really liked it when we
6 visited my grandparents in Florida. They made sure we were
7 matched right down to our underwear so that they could
8 keep Grandma and Grandpa tripped up.
9   Even as we got older, my parents kept up the routine. If
10 I'm being honest, I still liked all the attention it got us
11 everywhere we went. It was kind of like being a mini
12 celebrity. People even took our picture, and old ladies were
13 constantly hugging us or squeezing our cheeks. Some even
14 gave us money for candy or treats! Only with my parents'
15 permission, of course.
16   But now I guess you could say the novelty has worn
17 completely off. I am so sick of everyone thinking my sister
18 and I are just the same. Mirror images of each other in
19 every way. The proverbial two peas in a pod. Or some kind
20 of sci-fi futuristic clone. We are not the same. I am my own
21 person. I'm not my sister, and my sister is not me. We
22 aren't interchangeable where if you can't get one, just take
23 the other.
24   Everyone seems to think that we eat, breathe, and sleep
25 alike. That we think everything alike. That we have the
26 same dreams and goals. That our favorite foods, subjects,
27 movies, music, etc. are all the same. It's like a huge
28 surprise to them when they find out that my sister likes jazz

1 music and I like country, or that I love scary movies and my
2 sister is a big chicken. I just wish more people would get to
3 know us for who we are and not just what we appear to be.
4 I love my sister to pieces, but man, I sure wish she didn't
5 look just like me!

38. Picture Day — So Much Pressure

(Girl)

1 I've been standing here in front of my closet for two
2 hours now. As you can see from the pile here, I've tried on
3 at least fifteen different outfits. Nothing looks right. No
4 matter what I try on, it seems like I'm either trying too hard
5 or not trying hard enough. How do I get the perfect balance
6 in how I look for such an important day?

7 The outfit isn't the only problem either. Hair is just as
8 important. But again, I have to find the perfect balance. It
9 can't be too fancy or too plain, or people will judge me.
10 Should I wear it curly or is that overdoing it? Is straight
11 going to look like I didn't care at all? Am I supposed to look
12 like I don't care at all? I mean, this is the picture that people
13 will look at for the rest of their lives. When they sit down
14 with their kids to reminisce about their middle school years,
15 they will pull out their yearbooks, and there I will be.

16 I know it's silly, but there's so much pressure because
17 this one picture will represent my whole eighth grade year.
18 It will be in the yearbook forever. Friends will be old and
19 gray, looking back at those pictures. I don't want to be the
20 one that everyone points at and says, "Can you believe she
21 wore that?" Or "Look at that hair! What was she thinking?"
22 I know that's what happens too, because I've looked
23 through my parents' yearbooks, and some of those kids
24 look ridiculous! I don't want that to be me. I want to be one
25 of the ones that look cool now and even cooler twenty years
26 from now!

1   So if you don't mind, shut my door on the way out. I've
2 got about ten more outfits to try on! And then it's hair time.
3 I could easily be up all night!

39. That Is No Way to Wake Up

(Girl)

1   My best friend is treated like royalty. A real live princess
2   for sure. I always knew she was ultra-spoiled, but this is
3   more than just getting homemade cookies in her lunchbox
4   or new toys for absolutely no reason at all.
5   I spent the night there the other night and saw it all in
6   action. Her mother waits on her hand and foot. She didn't
7   even have to clear her own place after dinner! Later, when
8   Allie asked for cookies and her mother offered her store-
9   bought ones, Allie made a face and said, "No thanks." I
10 thought that was the end of it until I smelled fresh baked
11 chocolate chip cookies wafting through the house. Her mom
12 not only made her cookies, she had to go to the store first
13 to buy the ingredients. I couldn't believe it. At my house I
14 would've been happy just to have the store-bought ones! We
15 never have cookies!
16   But the real clincher was this morning, when it was time
17 to get up and go to soccer practice. Allie's mom came in
18 with freshly made muffins and orange juice on a tray. Then
19 she opened the blinds just a little and turned on a wave
20 machine. A wave machine! It was the most peaceful way to
21 wake up ever! And the muffins were amazing. Not even from
22 a box with dehydrated blueberry pieces!
23   Want to know how I wake up? With my mother slamming
24 open the door and yelling, *"Get up! We're late!"* And that's
25 on a good day. Most times she just yells up from downstairs
26 and doesn't even bother to climb up the steps. Allie says

1   her mom smothers her with all that attention and doing stuff

2   for her. But I tell you what — I could stand for a few days of

3   smothering! Isn't it my turn to be princess for a day?

40. Of Course I Want the Nice Car

(Guy)

1   The teachers have been hyping us up about the Annual
2   Life Fair for weeks now. Telling us how important it is to
3   make good decisions and treat the experience as a way to
4   learn real life skills. I don't really get how playing house with
5   some fake money is supposed to teach us anything. It's not
6   like reality at all. They're going to make us spin a wheel that
7   will decide our career and then based on that, they give us
8   a certain amount of money. How fair is that? I'm not lucky
9   at anything! I know I'm going to end up as a fast food
10 worker or a garbage truck driver. I'll have to figure out how
11 to live on minimum wage, and that's no fun at all! Who
12 wants to live like that?
13   Why can't I just tell them what I want to be? I already
14 know I'm going to be a surgeon and make tons of money.
15 I'm going to buy the biggest house I can find and drive the
16 sharpest sports car they make. I won't even have to worry
17 about money like this stupid Life Fair thing. I will have more
18 money than I need. So it's silly that they want me to walk
19 around with play money, trying to figure out how I'm going
20 to pay rent and put gas in a junker car that I would never
21 ever own in the first place.
22   Besides, even if I do spin the wheel and get a low-paying
23 job, I'm still getting a cool car. I just won't have a place to
24 live. I'll live in my car if I want! I'm a single guy ... well, at
25 least I *want* to be a single guy. But that's the other stupid
26 part. They're going to make me spin another wheel and

1   *make* me take a wife and kids. I could end up with as many
2   as six kids! *Six!* Who in their right mind has that many
3   children? I don't think they should force me to have kids if I
4   *know* I don't want them. Besides, do you have any idea how
5   expensive that would be? I'm not spending my hard-earned
6   money on that!
7   This whole thing is a big joke. I'm in charge of my life,
8   and if I'd rather have a super cool car and live alone. It's my
9   choice!

41. I Am Not Using That

(Guy)

1   I am not a germaphobe. Let's get that straight. That's
2 just overzealous and weird. What I am is normal. A normal
3 guy who knows disgusting when he sees it. And our
4 bathrooms at school are disgusting. Completely and utterly
5 disgusting. I don't see how they can expect us to use them.
6 I know they clean them every night, but kids my age are
7 pigs! I swear no one knows how to clean up after
8 themselves. They drop a paper towel on the floor, and they
9 just leave it there! I'd hate to see what their houses look
10 like.
11   It's not like I'm a total neat freak or anything, but come
12 on, people! Do we really have to live like this? Because of
13 the way they treat the place, I can't even use the bathroom
14 all day. You know how hard it is to go all day without using
15 the restroom? I won't even drink anything for breakfast or
16 at lunch because I don't dare risk it. A few times when I
17 haven't been able to hold it, I've actually faked being sick
18 so my mom would pick me up and take me home!
19   Yeah, I know that sounds obsessive, but if you saw what
20 I saw, you would know that I'm not exaggerating things in
21 the least. In fact, I may be underestimating how bad it really
22 is! Some kids don't even wash their hands. I've seen it! How
23 disgusting is that? For a while I wouldn't even touch things
24 in my classes. Things like the pencil sharpener or the
25 keyboard of the computer. But luckily the teacher finally
26 bought antibacterial wipes because of me! Those things are
27 a lifesaver, like for real! It makes me shudder to think of all
28 the germs running rampant around this place! I sure hope

1   it's better when I get to high school. Surely as these kids get
2   older, they'll understand the importance of not living like
3   animals!

42. Bedtimes Are for Babies

(Girl or Guy)

1   I have never understood why my parents think it's their
2 business or concern about what time I go to bed. Why do
3 they care if I go to school or soccer practice tired? Does that
4 affect them in any way? It sure doesn't affect me if my dad
5 goes to work after staying up late watching Monday Night
6 Football. Do I really care if he has to drink six cups of coffee
7 to get through the day?
8   The way I see it, it's my body, so shouldn't it be up to
9 me when I go to bed? Shouldn't I be the one deciding when
10 I'm tired and not my parents? I'm the one who will have to
11 fight being tired and the temptation to sleep through class.
12 I just don't see why it should matter to them.
13   Besides, none of my friends have bedtimes anymore.
14 They can stay up as late as they want. And watch what they
15 want on television too, but that's a whole other issue.
16 Bedtimes are for babies, not middle schoolers. I think I'm a
17 little too old to be treated like a toddler. It's like they still
18 think of me as a child and not a teenager who's practically
19 adult!
20   How can I convince my parents that I'm responsible
21 enough to handle going to bed at a reasonable time without
22 them telling me it's time to turn out the lights? I need them
23 to see that I am more than capable of making decisions like
24 that on my own. Maybe I should go on strike or something.
25 Stay up all night and show them that it's not the end of the
26 world if I don't get enough sleep. That it won't kill me if I'm

1   not asleep by nine o'clock. Yeah, it's a joke, I know! My best
2   friend's little sister goes to bed at ten p.m., and she's in
3   kindergarten! They've left me no other choice. It's time for
4   drastic measures. Tonight, I'm staying up all night long!

43. The Whole Truth and Nothing but the Truth ... Sort Of

(Girl or Guy)

1   I really don't see the harm in telling little white lies. They
2 don't hurt anyone. In fact, most of the time they do the
3 complete opposite. Like when my mom asks me if I like her
4 new haircut, and I really don't. Why would I tell her that I
5 don't? So why does everyone want me to feel guilty because
6 I like to stretch the truth a little?

7   It's not like I tell major lies or anything. It's just
8 sometimes I feel like I'm playing a part. Or telling a story. I
9 like to think of it as creative thinking. It's not like I cause
10 anyone any harm. I've never lied about anything that's
11 important.

12   I admit that sometimes it can get out of hand. One little
13 lie leads to another little lie, and then another and then
14 another, and it's easy to forget what the truth was. But that
15 doesn't mean I'm addicted to lying.

16   Most of the time, I never even get caught. Except the
17 other day I got caught red-handed, and man, was my mom
18 mad. See, I had taken a banana from the fruit bowl, and
19 after I opened it, I decided I really didn't want a banana. I
20 wanted an apple. So I threw the banana in the trash, got an
21 apple, and went into the living room. Well, my mom called
22 me back into the kitchen a few minutes later and asked me
23 if I'd eaten the banana. I could have told her that I didn't —
24 I mean, it's just a banana and I knew she wouldn't be *that*
25 mad that I'd wasted it — but I lied and told her I had. That's

1   when she pulled the banana out from behind her back and
2   asked me why I'd lied. Well, clearly it was because I didn't
3   know she had the evidence behind her back. She was really
4   mad that I lied straight to her face. She grounded me for a
5   whole week. Over a stupid banana! Only I guess it wasn't
6   really about the banana. But come on, did it really matter if
7   I ate the banana or not? Mom says I need to see the bigger
8   picture about building my character. I guess I understand
9   what she's saying, but it sure takes the fun out of things
10 when you have to tell the whole truth and nothing but the
11 truth!

44. My Mother Does Not Believe in Sick Days

(Girl or Guy)

1   My mother loves school days. I know this because I see
2   how happy she gets when summer is ending and my
3   brothers and sister and I are heading back to school. She is
4   almost giddy the first day back. I used to think that she was
5   just really excited for us, but I don't think it's that at all. I
6   think my mom likes having the house to herself. I think she
7   likes being home alone all day long. In fact, I am one
8   hundred percent sure of it, because once she gets us back
9   to school, she never lets us a miss a day. Ever.
10   I am dead serious. My mother's sick day policy has so
11   many rules that by the time she puts you through the paces,
12   you might as well just go on to school. She makes you take
13   your temperature, and no fever — and I mean a *real* fever of
14   over a hundred degrees at least — means no sick day. She
15   listens to you cough. No rattle, you are out the door. If your
16   stomach hurts but there's no evidence — yeah, I mean
17   puking or ... you know — then you get a couple of antacids
18   and a shove out the door. I think it takes an Act of Congress
19   to be able to stay home.
20   Then, if you feel sick at school, she'll make the nurse
21   check you out before she'll agree to come get you. You have
22   to have a broken bone or be seriously bleeding for her to
23   come sign you out and take you home. I even had a rash
24   one day and I was itching like crazy, but because I didn't
25   have a fever, my mom made me stay all day and then took
26   me to the doctor after school.

1   My friend is so lucky. She goes home all the time. She
2 can even go home for a headache. A headache! You can't
3 even see that. How does her mother know it's real? And yet
4 she gets to go home. Not even questioned when she gets
5 picked up. Geez, is it bad that I am hoping for a fever soon
6 so that I can get a day off?

45. Something's Fishy

(Guy)

1 I think something's going on with my dad, but no one's
2 telling me. Almost every weekend he says he's going on a
3 fishing trip with his buddies, but he never ever comes back
4 with fish. The first few times I didn't think anything of it,
5 because I figured they just ate everything they caught. But
6 he hasn't brought anything home in weeks now. And he's
7 never been gone fishing so much. Every weekend seems a
8 little excessive, doesn't it? He's hardly here all week, and
9 now he's gone all weekend too? Not to mention that he
10 hasn't brought me with him one time. He used to always
11 take me with him. Now he just makes excuses, saying that
12 his buddies need some guy time. What am I? A girl?
13 If that's not enough, my mom has been acting strange,
14 too. She's been crying a lot, and when I ask her why, she
15 says her aunt in California is really sick. I didn't even know
16 she *had* an aunt in California. I've sure never met her. It
17 *could* be true I guess, because California is really far away
18 and we never have that kind of money for traveling ... but
19 something just doesn't seem right.
20 They think I'm too young to pick up on it, I guess. They
21 think I won't see past the stupid fishing trips and a fake
22 sick aunt. Clearly they're trying to hide something from me.
23 But I'm not stupid. My parents are barely speaking to each
24 other. When my dad is home, he is never in the same room
25 as my mom. He's been eating dinner on the couch,
26 something my mom has never allowed in the past.
27 I wish they would just stop acting like nothing is wrong
28 and tell me what's going on. Why can't we all just sit down

1   and talk about it? Clearly their way isn't working. Besides,

2   what's the game plan when winter sets in? Is my dad going

3   to suddenly take up ice fishing?

46. Wasn't Me

(Girl or Guy)

1   Wow! I don't know what happened here over Christmas
2 break, but the school smells like death. I swear someone
3 has hidden rotting bodies down this hallway. How can they
4 expect us to put up with this? I feel like I need a gas mask
5 or something. It's making my eyes water!
6   Someone should contact the media. We shouldn't have
7 to go to school in these conditions. Oh my! It's just getting
8 worse and worse. And right by *my* locker too! Ewwww!
9 *(Holds nose.)* This is so disgusting! I think it's giving me a
10 headache! *(Mimes opening locker and jumping back.)*
11   Whoa! What the heck is in here? Oh ... oops ... Oh hey,
12 Mr. Mason! Yeah, it really stinks, doesn't it? *(Mimes*
13 *slamming locker.)* No ... it definitely wasn't coming from *my*
14 locker ... of course not ... must be Jarod's ... you know what
15 a slob he can be ... It wouldn't surprise me at all if he has
16 a whole carton of rotten eggs in there!
17   Yeah, I *know* it smells like it's coming from here ... but
18 I promise it's not! What? You want me to open it? There's
19 really no need ... I just had it open ... I think it's probably
20 from a couple of lockers down ...
21   Well, this is weird ... my locker won't open ... I think it's
22 stuck or something ... Yeah, I'm sure I have the combination
23 right ... huh ... well, maybe we can come check it later ... or
24 maybe you could check the ones farther down the row ... I'm
25 sure you'll find the culprit ... I bet someone just forgot their
26 lunch in there over Christmas break ... something
27 completely innocent ... something they really shouldn't get
28 in trouble for ... right?

47. Sadie Hawkins Is Not My Friend

(Girl)

1 I guess I'm just a good old-fashioned girl, because this
2 whole idea of girls asking boys out is just plain ridiculous!
3 Who came up with this idea in the first place? And who the
4 heck is Sadie Hawkins, and why is she messing things up?
5 Girls aren't supposed to ask boys to a dance. It's against
6 the laws of nature. Why would the school encourage
7 something like this? It's like they want to turn things upside
8 down.

9 Besides, how do you even ask someone out? Am I
10 supposed to do it in person? Over the phone? In a note?
11 Some of the girls are going all out. One girl even made up
12 a scavenger hunt, and at the end of the hunt, there is a huge
13 poster she made that asks the guy to the dance. Another
14 girl made homemade cookies and put a note — like a
15 fortune cookie — in one of them. Even if I wanted to ask a
16 guy out — which I don't — I wouldn't even know how to
17 compete with stuff like that. My big plan — if I *was* going to
18 do it — was to text the guy or maybe leave a note in his
19 locker. I sure wasn't going to go through all that. It's not
20 like I'm asking the guy to marry me or anything. Of course
21 that will probably be next, won't it? If this Sadie Hawkins
22 chick gets her way.

23 But what if I did ask someone ... and what if he said no?
24 How embarrassing would that be? Everyone would know! I
25 would never be able to face everyone again. There's a
26 reason that guys are supposed to do this. They have nerves

1   of steel. They don't get their feelings hurt. They can take the
2   rejection! This is all a mistake. I am not going to put myself
3   through this. So what if I miss one dance ... all this pressure
4   ... it's just not worth it!

48. Halloween Horror

(Girl or Guy)

1   I guess I didn't get the memo. The one where everyone
2 decided that dressing up for Halloween was too uncool to
3 do. So there I was, practically the only kid in school wearing
4 a costume. A Superman costume, to beat it all. Do you
5 know how embarrassing that was?
6   But what's wrong with everyone? We're not too old to
7 have fun. Besides, it's one of the only days we don't have to
8 wear our stupid uniforms. I don't care how silly it is or that
9 Halloween is only for little kids. This is our one day to relax
10 and have fun and not worry about our shirts being tucked
11 in. It's bad enough that most of us are too old to go trick-
12 or-treating. Now we have to give up dressing up too?
13   Sure there were a lot of restrictions on what we could
14 and couldn't wear ... no masks, no pajamas, no blood and
15 gore, etc. Not ideal. But come on. Be creative, people! There
16 are lots of options still open to us. By not dressing up, we
17 let them win. We let them take these opportunities to still
18 be kids out of us! We have plenty of time to be serious and
19 wear uniforms and work clothes. This is one day when we
20 get to still be young!
21   If we give up Halloween, what's next? Are we going to
22 give up Easter just because there are cute bunnies and
23 baskets of candy? Are those things too uncool also? What
24 about Valentine's Day? Or what about Christmas? I just
25 think that we have to hold tight to the few things we have
26 left. I'm not ready to grow up yet!

49. What Is That Noise?

(Girl or Guy)

1   I hate it when I'm trying to concentrate in class and I
2 hear someone's phone going off in their backpack. Even if
3 it's on silent mode, you can still hear it when it vibrates. It's
4 so annoying. And inconsiderate and rude.

5   So you should've seen me glaring at everyone around my
6 seat in class yesterday when someone's phone started
7 going off. I swear I stared down at least three different
8 students, trying to figure out who the culprit was. What I
9 couldn't understand was why they were staring back at me,
10 like I was the one doing something wrong. I don't even own
11 a cell phone. My parents won't let me have one yet.

12   But as everyone continued to stare at me, including the
13 teacher, I realized the sound *was* coming from my
14 backpack. I thought it must've been a prank or something.
15 Someone trying to get me in trouble. So once I figured out
16 which pocket the noise was coming from, I unzipped it to
17 find a beeping cell phone. My mother's cell phone. I knew it
18 the instant I saw the sparkly red case that looks like ruby
19 slippers. My mother's obsessed with *The Wizard of Oz*. What
20 I didn't know was *how* my mother's cell phone got in my
21 backpack. And what I also didn't know was my mother's
22 passcode to unlock the phone and turn the beeping off!

23   Meanwhile, everyone is staring at me, expecting me to
24 turn it off. I swear I wanted to throw it on the floor and
25 stomp on it until it stopped making noise. That's when Mr.
26 Arnold came to my desk and held out his hand. What else
27 could I do but hand it over? "It's not mine," I told him, but
28 I think he'd already figured that out when he saw me turning

1   it over and over, frantically trying to figure out how to turn
2   it off. I had no idea what he was going to do with it. That's
3   when he went to the mini fridge he keeps his lunch in and
4   shut my mother's phone in it! You could still hear the
5   beeping, but it was very faint. I expected him to give me
6   detention or something, but he just opened his book and
7   started teaching. I guess the next time I hear a phone going
8   off, I won't be so judgmental. In fact, I may even be
9   sympathetic!

50. Hurts Him More Than It Hurts Me

(Guy)

1   You're not going to believe me when I tell you that I think
2   my school basketball coach is a really great guy. Especially
3   given the fact that he cut me and twelve other guys from the
4   team last week. I could tell when he had to make the cuts
5   that he didn't really want to. As cliché as it sounds, it really
6   *did* seem to hurt him more than it hurt me. Not that I wasn't
7   crushed, because I was. Not making the team now means
8   that I probably won't make the high school team either
9   which pretty much halts all my dreams of being a
10   professional basketball star. And what guy doesn't dream of
11   being a future NBA star? Especially a really tall guy like me.
12   I will easily hit six feet in a few years. So it was pretty
13   devastating to hear the news that I'd been cut.
14   But you could see that it really bothered Coach. He
15   seemed really upset. I guess I never stopped to think of that
16   side of things before. How hard it would be to be the one
17   who has to give the bad news like that. To let some kids
18   down and hurt their feelings. Who wants to be *that* guy? I
19   would hate to be in his shoes. It's not his fault that thirty
20   kids tried out for the team. It's not like he can keep every
21   guy who tried out on the team. That would be ridiculous.
22   Because even if he did, we wouldn't all get to play. We'd be
23   sitting on the bench all the time, and what fun is that? I'd
24   rather be cut and move on to something else than sit here
25   watching my friends play all season.
26   More than missing playing basketball, I think I'll miss
27   Coach. He really seemed to care about all of us. And he was

1 always being encouraging and pushing us to do our best
2 without being mean. In fact, he's the only coach I've had
3 who actually didn't yell all through practice. I guess I can see
4 why so many guys tried out this year. Everyone likes being
5 around him. Maybe I won't give up on my basketball career.
6 I'll just try harder so that next year when Coach has to give
7 the cuts, I won't be one of them!

51. Almost There

(Girl or Guy)

1 My mom says the only way we can move on from what's
2 happened is to forgive that girl. And I know I should. I know
3 deep, deep down that I should. Because the anger I have for
4 her is eating me up inside. But how can I? How can I forgive
5 the girl who hurt my brother?
6   He wasn't doing anything wrong. He was exactly where
7 he was supposed to be. Playing with sidewalk chalk out in
8 our driveway. He wasn't even close to the road. All she had
9 to do was stay on the road. Pay attention to what she was
10 doing. Is that so hard? Isn't that what you agree to when
11 you get your license? When they let you get behind the
12 wheel of a car that can kill someone in the blink of an eye?
13   Want to know why the girl hit my brother? Want to know
14 *why* she wasn't paying attention to driving? She was
15 texting. That's right. Sending an all-important text to her
16 boyfriend that she was "Almost there." *Almost there.* Two
17 words. Two words that could've waited. Did it really matter
18 so much if her boyfriend knew she was *almost there?* He
19 couldn't just wait and see her drive up? Was knowing she
20 was *almost there* going to change their lives in any way? No!
21 But it sure changed my brother's. My innocent little brother
22 who never hurt anyone in his life. It changed the course of
23 *his* life forever.
24   Now, because of her, my brother can't walk. Ever. My
25 little brother who loved to ride his tricycle, run around
26 catching bubbles, play hide and seek, and chase our dog.
27 My little brother who won't walk at his own graduation. Or
28 down the aisle when he gets married.

1   *(Really loudly)* **Almost there?** *(Much softer)* **Almost** ...
2   **there ... I sure hope it was really that important ...**

52. Last Place

(Girl or Guy)

1   My dad is so unreasonable. He thinks that just because
2   he was an all-star athlete in middle and high school that I
3   should be too. My mom's just as bad. I think they're
4   embarrassed by me. The fact that I never even come close to
5   winning. But it's just not going to happen. I guess I *could* be
6   a winner if I wanted to. But do you have any idea how much
7   work it takes to be number one? How much time you have to
8   spend practicing? Why would I want to spend all my time
9   getting in shape just so I can win a stupid ribbon or trophy?
10   I just don't even get what the big deal is. *Someone* has
11   to come in last. Why can't it or why shouldn't it be me?
12   Truth is ... I help make the other kids look better. I let the
13   real stars shine through. Isn't that just as important?
14   Besides, isn't there some kind of saying about "the first
15   shall be last and the last shall be first"? So maybe it's a
16   good thing that I take the last spot.
17   Why *should* I think I am above coming in last place? Why
18   do my parents think I am above it? Do they really put
19   themselves up above all the other parents to think that their
20   kid absolutely can't come in dead last? Isn't that so
21   superior of them? So smug? So conceited? Of course it is!
22   There is *no* reason why I can't be last.
23   So who cares what they post on the board today. I'm
24   totally fine with coming in last place ... oh, wait ... they're
25   putting up the scores now ... What? Wait! That can't be
26   right! Wow! I didn't come in last! Oh, thank goodness. I'm
27   so glad I'm not last. No one really wants to be last. I think
28   maybe I should practice a little more this week.

53. Cafeteria Crud

(Girl or Guy)

1   Want to know what I just heard? You won't even believe
2   it! I researched it on the Internet, and it's true. I can't
3   believe people actually know about this stuff and are OK
4   with it! When I told my dad, he just shrugged like it's no big
5   deal. Of course, he was watching a game, so who knows if
6   he really even heard what I said. But you'd think a thing like
7   this would certainly get his attention! Doesn't he care at all
8   what his kids are eating? Shouldn't he be a little more upset
9   that we're being fed bugs at school?

10   That's right. Did you know that there is a certain
11   percentage of bugs and hair that are *allowed* in school food?
12   In *any* restaurant or processed food? That's right. *Allowed.*
13   Isn't that disgusting? But now that I think about it, I'm
14   pretty sure I *have* seen cockroach legs sticking out of my
15   burger. And now that I know it's a distinct possibility, I
16   probably have for sure!

17   Who makes up the rules on this? How can even one hair
18   or one insect leg or body part be *allowed* in my food?
19   Shouldn't they have stricter rules on that? Why would
20   anyone ever agree to standards like this? It's not like we live
21   in a Third World country or something. This is America. We
22   have the FDA — the Food and Drug Administration — to
23   make sure that things like this don't happen.

24   I swear I'm never going to eat anywhere except my
25   house ever again! And I'm bringing my lunch to school from
26   now on. My dad said I'm being silly, that everyone has to eat
27   a pound of dirt before they die. Well, that may be true, but I
28   do *not* have to eat a pound of bugs!

54. A House Divided Cannot Stand

(Girl or Guy)

1   Siblings are *supposed* to fight, right? Isn't that just part
2 of the natural way of things? Penny is supposed to get on
3 my nerves and I'm supposed to get on hers. We don't mean
4 anything real by it. Like I wouldn't really want her to get hit
5 by a bus like I yelled at her yesterday. And I know she
6 wouldn't really want me to fall off the Empire State Building.
7 It's just stupid things we say when we're mad at each other.
8 It's all completely harmless.
9   So I don't get why our parents are making such a huge
10 deal about it. Don't they remember what it's like to be
11 aggravated by a sibling? But they say that we've gotten out
12 of hand. That we are too mean and disrespectful to each
13 other.
14   They've decided to institute what they call a "Nice Law."
15 We are only allowed to say nice things to each other.
16 Anything that comes out of our mouths has to be
17 supportive, loving, caring, etc., or we're supposed to not say
18 anything at all. If we don't obey and say mean things
19 anyway, we have to draw a slip from the punishment jar,
20 which includes all kinds of things from writing "I'm sorry for
21 being mean" two hundred times to cleaning all the toilets in
22 the house. Personally I think they put more chores than
23 anything in that jar because ultimately they just want the
24 house to get cleaned.
25   They *know* we can't abide by rules like this. It's
26 impossible. *So* unrealistic. I'm not even supposed to *like* my

1 sister right now, am I? Isn't this breaking some kind of
2 cosmic law? How can I get my parents to lift this "Nice Law"
3 and let us be normal kids?

55. Chores Are Not Just for Girls

(Girl)

1   Home is the one place you think that you'll always be
2   treated fairly. Equally. It's not supposed to be like out in the
3   world, where bad things happen to good people and life is
4   unfair and sometimes cruel and all the things they say like
5   that. So if that's true, then why am I stuck with a full-page
6   chore list, and my brother has barely anything to do? He
7   doesn't have to do half the stuff that I have to do! They act
8   like him mowing the lawn is the hardest thing on earth! Well,
9   I'll trade with him any day! We have a *riding* mower. How
10 hard can that be?
11   You would think that my parents would love us equally.
12 But clearly they don't, because how is this fair in the least?
13 I feel like I'm the Cinderella in the family and he's the Prince
14 Charming. He waltzes around here like he owns the place
15 and I'm the hired help. Why wouldn't he? He knows he's got
16 it lucky. He knows that being a guy around here is just like
17 being royalty.
18   It's all because of the way my mom treats my dad. She
19 waits on him hand and foot. He never even cleans his own
20 place after dinner. And if he's watching television and wants
21 something to drink, he just hollers at my mom and she gets
22 it for him! Like he doesn't have two legs that work. My mom
23 is always doing things for him. It's so unfair. And now she's
24 expecting me to be the same way. Like the guys in this
25 family are just guests and don't have to help out with
26 anything.

1   I tell you what, when I pick a husband, I'm picking a guy
2 who knows how to cook, clean, and do his own laundry! If
3 he can't do those things, he can forget about being my
4 husband! I am not going to be Cinderella forever.

56. I Love Rainy Days

(Girl or Guy)

1   They are predicting a whole week of stormy, dreary,
2 rainy weather, and I couldn't be happier! I know it's kind of
3 weird but I love weather like this, and we hardly ever get
4 such a great forecast! I just hope it doesn't pass us by. I
5 could really use these days to get caught up on my sleep.
6 Rainy days are perfect for napping, thinking, reading, and
7 just plain quiet. But nobody seems to get that. They think
8 that just because you like the rainy weather that you must
9 be all doom and gloom. But I'm nothing like that.

10   I may not be like my perky sister, who is all full of
11 sunshine and rainbows, but I'm no Eeyore. Just because I
12 don't get giddy over a beautiful day, doesn't mean that I'm
13 full of darkness. Still, people look at me funny, and yet
14 everyone loves her. Scratch that. Everyone *adores* her. She
15 smiles nonstop, wears ribbons in her hair, and giggles like
16 a babbling brook. *All the time.*

17   They see me as the dark cloud ... the serious, pensive,
18 and full-of-thought sibling who would be happy if the sun
19 never shone again. Which isn't totally untrue, although I
20 know I'd miss it some. I just prefer the gray days. Not
21 because they're dreary, but because they're peaceful. Why
22 do rainy days get such a bad rap? Those are the only days
23 when you can sit around and do nothing and not feel guilty.
24 Besides, rain brings life. Ask any farmer. So why shouldn't
25 we celebrate these days just as much as the blue sky ones?

26   All I know is that I can't wait for the rain to come. I say
27 bring on those rainy days!

57. Old Man, Put Your Shirt On

(Girl or Guy)

1 Have you ever seen something that you wish you could
2 unsee? Something that makes you wish you could either rip
3 your eyes out or pour bleach in them or something? Yeah,
4 I'm talking bad. Not car-wreck bad, like blood and gore bad.
5 I can handle that kind of stuff. In fact, I love scary, gory
6 movies. The gorier the better. No, this is nothing like that.
7 This ... is disgusting.

8   Don't believe me? Take a look at that! That's my
9 neighbor, Old Man Harrison. Do you see how gross that is?
10 And he is out there every day for hours just like that! Mows
11 his yard that way. Gets the mail that way. Uses the Weed
12 Eater that way. Does his gardening that way. Sits on his
13 porch that way. Day in and day out, I have to see the old
14 man that way.

15   Doesn't he ever look in a mirror? How can he keep his
16 shirt off like that all the time? I'm beginning to think the
17 man doesn't even *own* a shirt. His skin is sagging so badly,
18 it looks like it's melting off him! I think he has more rolls
19 than a Shar Pei — those dogs with the major wrinkles.

20   Doesn't he know that so much sun on all that skin has
21 to be some kind of major skin cancer risk? He looks all
22 leathery, and that can't be good. It's disgusting, if nothing
23 else. I guess it's that he cares so little about what everyone
24 thinks. I would die of embarrassment before I'd be seen like
25 that. But good ol' Harry doesn't seem to care. That's one of
26 the good things about being older than dirt, I guess. You

1 stop caring what people think about you. I just wish he
2 could care a little bit every now and then and put his shirt
3 on!

58. Raking for Dr. Berry

(Guy)

1   I can't wait until I am old enough to drive. Then I'm
2 going to get a real job where I can get paid fairly for the job
3 I do. I've been mowing, raking lawns, and shoveling
4 driveways for years now. Most people are pretty fair about
5 what they pay me. Then there's Dr. Berry. If my parents
6 didn't make me, I wouldn't even rake his yard anymore.

7   Every time I do it, I make sure to get every stinking leaf.
8 I go over that yard with a fine-tooth comb. I know how he is.
9 He loves bringing me back and showing me a spot that I've
10 missed. Sometimes I swear he puts the leaves there
11 himself. Like I'm being framed or something.

12   It's like a game with him. I think he likes the power he
13 has over me. He knows he doesn't have to pay me until the
14 job is done. So he drags it out just to show me who's in
15 charge. Doesn't he realize that the yard can never be done
16 a hundred percent when the leaves are still falling? It's not
17 my fault that more leaves come down in the backyard while
18 he's inspecting the front! It's unreasonable to make me feel
19 like I haven't done a good job. Can't he see the blisters on
20 my hands? I'm a hard worker. I don't deserve to be
21 scrutinized like that.

22   But that's not even the worst part. The good doctor is
23 cheap. Not on the stuff he owns, like his million-dollar
24 mansion or fancy silver sports car. Oh no. He's not cheap
25 when it comes to that. Want to know what he pays me?
26 After all that work and criticism, he only pays me ten
27 dollars. For the whole yard! Next year I'm waiting until
28 winter sets in, then I'll get all the leaves the first time, and
29 maybe Dr. Berry will actually pay me what I deserve!

59. Sneaky Pete

(Guy)

1   I am easily the next James Bond double-oh-seven.
2 Spying is something I love to do. When I was younger, I had
3 a spy kit and everything. It was pretty cool. And even
4 though I've outgrown fake spy badges and fingerprint kits, I
5 haven't outgrown spying. I have become so good at it that
6 my family never even knows I am there. I have found the
7 best hiding places all around my house where I can watch
8 and listen to things as they are going on. And no one ever
9 catches me. I think my spy name will actually be Sneaky
10 Pete. Because I'm extra sneaky and because ... well, my
11 name is Pete. Clever, huh?
12   You wouldn't believe the things I've found out over the
13 years. One Christmas I knew every single gift that was
14 under the tree. That actually wasn't as cool as I thought it
15 would be ... so I don't sneak at Christmastime anymore. I
16 figured out that I actually like surprises more than knowing
17 what I'm getting. Same about birthday time. Once I found
18 out about a surprise birthday party for me. That kind of
19 ruined it, so I definitely stay away from my hiding places
20 around June, too.
21   But some stuff I've found out is really cool. Like how
22 proud my dad was of me when my team won first place in
23 the tournament. Sure, he'd told me too. But hearing him
24 brag on the phone with my grandma was pretty awesome.
25 Another time, I heard him tell my uncle that he thought I
26 was going to be over six feet tall! And that maybe I'd play
27 pro basketball!

1   I've heard some bad stuff too. Like fights between my
2 parents that I know they didn't want me to know about. Or
3 about money problems when my dad got laid off. It's not
4 stuff I really want to hear, but once I'm in position, it's hard
5 to come out. Not without getting caught anyway, which a
6 good spy never does!
7   Besides, you gotta take the good with the bad. If I gave
8 up spying, I never would've heard my sister on the phone
9 this week talking about how she's failing chemistry and
10 skipped class three times in one week! I have definitely got
11 to be around when my parents find out about that one!

60. Exercise Enthusiast Is an Understatement

(Girl or Guy)

1   My mother is obsessed with working out. Do you know
2   what she did the other day? She ran to the restaurant where
3   we ate dinner. And then she ran back home while the rest
4   of us all rode in the car. Want to know how far that
5   restaurant is from our house? Ten miles! Isn't that some
6   kind of crazy? Who runs to and from a restaurant? Isn't that
7   like an oxymoron or something? Running to go eat? Except
8   she barely ate anything anyway, so it didn't really count.

9   It's like she never stops working out. Even when she's
10 vacuuming or sweeping, she's got some kind of weights
11 strapped to her legs or her arms. She never sits down. At
12 night when we watch television, she's doing wall sits or
13 crunches or — and this one is the most annoying —
14 jumping jacks! Do you have any idea how distracting it is
15 to watch a show while someone is doing jumping jacks?
16 The whole house shakes!

17   She hardly cooks anymore, either. She is doing this
18 "pure" thing where everything she eats has to have three
19 ingredients or less. She prefers only one. That's right: one
20 ingredient, which means a fruit or vegetable or maybe if
21 we're lucky, some kind of lean meat. That's fine if that's
22 what she wants to eat, but do we have to suffer too? I'm not
23 a rabbit, and I refuse to eat like one. There's nothing wrong
24 with good old country cooking, like a nice fat meatloaf with
25 mashed potatoes and gravy. Just ask my grandma. She's in
26 her seventies and she doesn't care about some fad diet that

1   everyone's trying.

2   Want to know what my mom has done now? She's
3   signed our whole family up for a 5K. A 5K! That's over three
4   miles! I think it's time my dad put his foot down. This
5   craziness has got to stop! Workout Mom needs to retire!

61. Yellow Dog Award

(Girl or Guy)

1   I don't see what the big deal is. Everyone is acting like
2   it's the Academy Awards or something huge like that. It's
3   just a stupid class award. It's definitely no reason to get all
4   keyed up and start acting crazy. That's all my friends have
5   been talking about lately. Trying to figure out who's going to
6   get Mr. Wright's Yellow Dog Award.
7   Why would he even call it that? It's not like history has
8   anything to do with dogs in the first place. Why would a
9   yellow dog be the mascot for our class? He even makes
10 videos that star the stupid ratty old pooch. I guess I just
11 don't understand the reasoning behind everyone clamoring
12 to get an award that's named after a stuffed animal. But Mr.
13 Wright's been hyping it up all week. Even now, he's making
14 a huge production out of it. He's been dragging out who's
15 getting the award for over fifteen minutes now.
16   The suspense is killing me ... not! I'd be so embarrassed
17 if he called my name. How lame would that be to tell
18 everyone that I'd won the Yellow Dog Award. That I was the
19 student who Mr. Wright thought went above and beyond
20 throughout the year. That I was the student who exemplified
21 integrity and honesty and helpfulness toward others. That I,
22 over everyone else, showed a willingness to listen and an
23 eagerness to learn. About history, no less! How lame would
24 that be? Right?
25   So of course I don't care whose name Mr. Wright calls,
26 I just don't want it to be me. Wait ... why is everyone
27 looking at me? Did he really just say my name? Like for
28 real? Like I really just won the Yellow Dog Award?

1   Oh wow. Thank you, Mr. Wright. Gosh. I had no idea.
2   Wow. This is really super cool ...

62. A High IQ Doesn't Always Mean Smart

(Girl or Guy)

1   There are people who have common sense and people
2 who have book smarts. I like to think that I have a little bit
3 of both. I'm not the ultra-student who makes straight As all
4 the time, but I'm not flunking out either. And when it comes
5 to problem-solving a way out of a situation, I'm a real pro.
6 That's where the common sense comes in. I know my
7 parents have always appreciated that about me, but let's be
8 honest. They've *loved* my brother's high IQ and consistent
9 four-point-oh GPA.

10   At least they did until the other day. Now I think they
11 may be appreciating my averageness just a little bit more.
12 See, my brother is in high school, and he's taking some
13 really hard classes this year that count toward college. That
14 is, they *would* count toward college if he passes what they
15 call an AP test. The test itself should've been a piece of
16 cake for my brother. He's never struggled with grades his
17 entire life. He even got a thirty-two on his ACT for college
18 entrance. So I guess no one was really concerned when he
19 left to take the test last Saturday.

20   But that's when my brother's lack of common sense
21 came into play. See, apparently the test ran longer than it
22 was supposed to, and he was still waiting to record the oral
23 section of his foreign language test. He was supposed to
24 speak in French for approximately ten minutes on a subject
25 they would give him. Well, someone at the school messed
26 up and didn't bring enough recorders, so it was taking way

1 longer than it was supposed to. Apparently my brother was
2 getting hungry. And so were three of his genius friends.
3 Want to know what they did? They left to go get food. Even
4 though it clearly says you are *not* allowed to leave the
5 testing site. Now they are all in big trouble, and they may
6 not even count his scores on his test! Which means *no*
7 college credit for those classes! Boy, are my parents mad!
8 How could he be so smart and yet so dumb? I sure hope that
9 burrito was worth it, 'cause it will end up costing him about
10 a thousand dollars in lost test fees and college credit!

63. Wish I'd Had This Life

(Girl or Guy)

1   Here I am stuck in this house, day after day, night after
2 night, and I just can't take it anymore. I can't believe how
3 mouthy kids are today! If I spoke to my parents like that, I
4 would've been eating a bar of soap every night. And what's
5 up with kids keeping those things in their ears the whole
6 time their parents are talking to them, anyway? How can
7 they even hear what they're saying? They're just so
8 disrespectful! I wish I could move on, but I can't. For some
9 reason, I'm stuck here. I guess for eternity. Maybe this is my
10 eternal punishment for the trouble I caused my own parents.
11 Who knows? But if my parents could see kids today, they'd
12 be soooo happy to have me back! Well ... if they were still
13 alive, that is.

14   And the complaining! Do you have any idea what this
15 kid complains about in a given day? He acts like waiting two
16 minutes at the microwave for his popcorn to come out is a
17 lifetime. Two minutes! We didn't even have microwaves
18 when I was alive. That is like the most awesome thing ever.
19 The only way we could make popcorns was in a pan with oil
20 and kernels. Do you know how long that took? And half the
21 time it stuck to the pan and burned. It definitely didn't taste
22 as good as popcorn today smells. It's enough to make a
23 ghost go crazy.

24   This kid has a cell phone, a laptop, an iPad, all kinds of
25 video game equipment, and yet you know what he argued
26 about the other day? How mean his mom was for not buying
27 him the latest video game. And it's not even his birthday or
28 a holiday! We never got presents for absolutely no reason.

1   Heck, we were lucky to get presents when it *was* our
2   birthday or a holiday. But kids today are so entitled. This kid
3   doesn't even have a job. Yeah, I know he's only twelve, but
4   where's his paper route? Why isn't he chopping wood or
5   mowing lawns or something?
6   All I know is ... whatever I did to get stuck here, I'd undo
7   in a heartbeat! I just can't take today's kids anymore!

64. She Isn't Deaf — She's Just from Mexico

(Girl or Guy)

1   I knew I should've never asked Marissa to our house
2   after school. My mother tends to overdo things when she's
3   trying to impress someone, and I guess the idea of having
4   an exchange student from Mexico over was enough to make
5   her go into full crazy mode.

6   I opened the door to red and green banners all over the
7   living room. Yeah, Mexico's flag colors. She even took the
8   image of the flag and had it transferred onto a cake. But
9   that's not all. She had Latino music playing on the stereo
10 and some kind of food laid out on the table that I can only
11 assume was a Mexican recipe. I know she was only trying to
12 make Marissa feel comfortable, but it was all so over the
13 top!

14 Marissa was gracious and acted like it was totally
15 normal that my mother is crazy. It was so embarrassing,
16 and I thought it couldn't get any worse. And then it did. My
17 mother opened her mouth. She started talking to Marissa in
18 this really loud, slow, annoying voice, like the girl was
19 partially deaf or something!

20 Marissa looked as confused as I was. Which I guess is
21 why my mother thought she couldn't understand plain
22 English, so she started making hand gestures, using
23 ridiculous impromptu sign language. Of course that just
24 stunned both of us into deeper silence! My mother was like
25 an act in the circus! So when we didn't respond to her
26 antics, she pulled out the big guns. A huge flipchart with

1   markers where she started drawing what she was trying to
2   say. It was like a big game of Pictionary!
3   It was all so humiliating. I don't think Marissa could call
4   her exchange family fast enough to come get her! And you
5   should've seen my mother's face when she did it in *perfect*
6   *English.*

65. Fake Shoes Stink

(Girl)

1　　Let me just state for the record that off-brand items are
2　not "just as good" as the name brand stuff, as my mother
3　would like me to believe. In fact, off-brand items stink.
4　Literally. I had begged my mom for a pair of Tom's for school
5　this year, but she absolutely refused to buy them for me.
6　Said it was ridiculous to pay that much money for a pair of
7　shoes when they made ones that looked just like them for
8　a whole lot cheaper price. She wouldn't even waver when I
9　told her how the Tom's company donated a pair of shoes to
10　needy kids with every purchase. I thought for sure that
11　would convince her that they were worth the price. I would
12　get something, and so would a needy kid. How could she
13　turn down that kind of logic?
14　　But she wasn't buying. Literally. Instead, she brought
15　me home a pair of near-identical Tim's. Same red color that
16　I wanted in the name brand shoes. I will admit that they
17　looked very, very similar. And these were half the price.
18　They didn't have the logo that I wanted on them, but even I
19　had to admit that they were a pretty close copycat. But after
20　a week I figured out why they were so cheap. The off-brand
21　stunk! And I mean physically stunk! I think it was from
22　either the cheap fabric or the cheap rubber they used on the
23　soles.
24　　My mom tried to blame my feet! Even bought me
25　deodorant foot spray, but it didn't work. The smell was
26　horrible! I couldn't even wear them out anymore. I was too
27　embarrassed, so Mom had to buy me another pair of shoes.
28　Sneakers this time, so that I'd have something to wear to

1   school. By the time she paid for those, she could've easily
2   bought me the name brand shoes in the first place! I'm
3   hoping that this taught her a valuable lesson, because for
4   Christmas, I'm asking for a Michael Kors purse!

66. Supersize Me

(Girl or Guy)

1   Did you know that New York City is trying to ban
2   supersized drinks? They're going to limit drink sizes to
3   sixteen ounces. What if I'm thirstier than that? What if I
4   have a long drive in front of me, and I need more caffeine
5   than that? Why would the government think it's any of their
6   business what size drink people want? Isn't that called
7   government overreach or something? Isn't that the
8   government putting their nose in business that doesn't
9   belong to them?
10 How can there be a law about what a person can drink?
11 And do they really think that will stop obesity? Do they
12 really think that the people who overeat or indulge in
13 calories they can't afford aren't going to find a way to get
14 those extra calories anyway? Have they ever heard of a
15 refill? What's the difference? And how is it their business
16 anyway?
17 If they think they can do this, what's next? Are they
18 going to tell me what I can eat? What I can wear? What I
19 should study when I go to college? Maybe they're going to
20 tell me where I can live. Or what kind of pet I can own. Or
21 maybe they'll tell me what kind of car I can drive. What if
22 they decide that we all have to own electric cars only? They
23 could say that it is to save the earth and everyone's
24 responsibility. But what about the people who can't afford
25 to buy one? Will they force us to? Is that what this nation
26 has become? A nation that dictates to the people what they
27 should and shouldn't do in their everyday ordinary lives?

1   Listen up, people! Drink bans are only the beginning. We
2   can't let the government take control of our lives. Stand up
3   and be heard! Do not give up your right to buy supersize!

67. Is It Tuesday Yet?

(Girl or Guy)

1   Do you sometimes forget when you're watching a
2   television show that it's not really real? That the people are
3   just actors and that none of it is really happening? I mean,
4   I know everyone gets lost in a show or movie at some point,
5   but I'm, like, totally hooked on this show, and it's making
6   me crazy! I can't stop thinking about it. I actually lose sleep
7   over it. I keep worrying about what's going to happen next,
8   if my two favorite characters are going to fall in love, who's
9   going to die ... the list goes on.
10   My whole week is geared around this show. It only airs
11   on Tuesday nights, so you'd think I could let it go the other
12   six nights, but I can't. In my mind it's always, "One more
13   night until my show comes on." Or as soon as it's over that
14   night, all I can think about is the next Tuesday and how long
15   it's going to take to get here. I've totally lost that "live in the
16   moment" attitude I used to have. Now everything revolves
17   around Tuesday night! And if the show isn't on for stupid
18   things like Presidential updates, the Olympics, or ball
19   games, I practically go ballistic!
20   I tape every episode. Sometimes I watch it more than
21   once ... OK ... all the time I watch them more than once.
22   Usually three or four times! Isn't that nuts? I really feel like
23   I *know* these people. That I care about them as if they were
24   part of my family. I know it's not normal, but I can't stop
25   myself from obsessing about it. I actually blame the writers
26   and the actors! If they weren't so stinking good, it wouldn't
27   seem so true to life! So real! So compelling! They have a
28   hook, like, *every* episode! It's like they *want* to torture me!

1   I know you think it's just my favorite television show.
2 But it's not. It's my *life*.

68. Family Picture Fiasco

(Girl or Guy)

1   I don't know why my mom gets her hopes up every year
2 that the outcome is going to be different. It never is. She
3 spends all this time color-coordinating our outfits, making
4 sure that every outfit is clean and pressed and that all of our
5 hair is trimmed and styled. Then she puts us all in front of
6 a camera, and click! Disaster begins.

7   My brother Sam does *not* know how to smile. He
8 doesn't. I really didn't think that was something you had to
9 learn how to do, but apparently it is, because at age seven,
10 he hasn't got a clue. His mouth curves all weirdly — or
11 rather it doesn't curve at all. It's more like an awkward line
12 across his face. It's the goofiest thing you've ever seen.

13   Then there's my sister Allison. She doesn't know how to
14 keep her eyes open to save her life. Every time she hears
15 "Three!" — as in one, two, three! — her eyes immediately
16 close or go into squint mode. We seriously do *not* have a
17 picture of her with her eyes open.

18   My older brother Jordan is the real troublemaker,
19 though. As soon as Mom and Dad get into place where they
20 can't see what he's doing, his arm shoots up to put horns
21 on someone's head, or a peace sign, or hang loose, or
22 whatever else he can make with his arms and fingers. Which
23 of course gets all of us tickled, and so instead of looking all
24 proper like Mom wants, we're all doubled over, giggling
25 hysterically.

26   I think Mom should just accept that she's never going
27 to get the family portrait she sees in her head. What she's
28 going to get is what she gets every year — a great snapshot
29 of who we really are. And what can be better than that?

69. Dear Diary

(Girl or Guy)

1   Dear Diary,

2   Today was the absolute worst day of my entire life. I
3 know that may not sound that impressive since I'm only
4 eleven years old, but believe me, it is. I don't think I will ever
5 forget it for as long as I live.

6   I should've known something was wrong because Corky
7 is always at the foot of my bed, sound asleep, snoring like
8 an old man when it's time for me to get ready for school. But
9 I guess I didn't really even stop and think about it. Isn't it
10 weird how some things become so routine that you don't
11 even realize when things aren't the way they usually are? So
12 I got ready as usual and didn't even think about the fact
13 that Corky wasn't at my side when I headed down the stairs.

14   And that's when I saw him. Down at the bottom. His
15 body was contorted and jerking around, and at first I
16 thought he was just dreaming, maybe running after a rabbit
17 or something. As I got to him though, I knew something was
18 wrong. His eyes were weird and his tongue was hanging
19 loosely out of his mouth. I screamed for my dad and he
20 came running. It only took a few seconds for my dad to
21 scoop Corky up in his arms and rush him out to the car. I
22 ran with them and we were at the vet's office in no time. The
23 vet took him behind the swinging doors immediately. We
24 weren't allowed to go back with him.

25   I still thought it was going to be OK. We had him exactly
26 where he needed to be. Got him help as fast as we could.
27 Dad kept telling me that Corky was strong. That he would
28 be all right.

1   But I knew the minute the vet walked back through the
2 swinging doors that my dad and I were wrong. Corky was
3 not going to be OK. In fact, Corky was dead.
4   Now here I am, back in my bed, and I don't think I will
5 ever be able to fall asleep. How can I without the weight of
6 Corky on my feet? I will miss my best friend forever. Good
7 night, Corky.

70. Lucy Linebacker

(Girl)

1   I wish my mother had never named me after my Great
2 Aunt Lucille. It's not that I have anything against the
3 woman, or even the name itself, but maybe if I didn't have
4 the name Lucy, the kids at school wouldn't be calling me
5 "Lucy Linebacker." Why couldn't she have named me after
6 my grandmother Pamela? "Pamela Linebacker" just doesn't
7 have the same ring to it, does it? Maybe they would've left
8 me alone.

9   I can't blame it totally on the name, though, because
10 certainly other things could go with Lucy. Like "Lovely Lucy"
11 or "Laughing Lucy" or "Little Lucy." But of course they
12 would never call me any of those. Mostly because I'm not
13 lovely, I definitely don't laugh a lot, and I am certainly not
14 *little*. Hence the name "Lucy Linebacker."

15   See, my shoulders are about as broad as a barn. I really
16 look like I have been lifting weights — or maybe houses —
17 my whole life. My back is bigger than my father's! I swear it
18 is! It's so awful. A girl is supposed to be petite and little.
19 Not look like a football player!

20   The boys at school actually asked if I was trying out for
21 the football team. And I think they were serious! They knew
22 I would be the best defensive tackle they've ever seen.

23   My grandmother says there's nothing wrong with husky
24 girls. *Husky girls.* Yeah. That's something everyone wants to
25 hear! She might as well have called me *big boned* —which
26 of course I am.

27   I am so jealous of my friend Melissa. She is petite like
28 a stinking china doll. She is literally only four feet tall and

1 eighty pounds soaking wet. Her feet are so tiny that she still
2 wears kid shoes. I haven't worn kid shoes since I started
3 walking practically! She says it's awful being so tiny. That
4 everyone treats her like a baby. Well, I say walk a mile in
5 these shoulders, sista!

71. Mr. Sampson the Spitter

(Girl)

1   I hate assigned seating. My last name is Adams, and I
2   always get stuck in the front row of class, because of course
3   no teacher can come up with an original way to arrange the
4   class. They always go back to good old alphabetical. Just
5   once I wish they would try something else. Or maybe just
6   do the alphabet backwards — what a novel idea!
7   But no. I have to get stuck on the front row. Every time.
8   And this class is the worst, because Mr. Sampson is the
9   hands-down worst ever talk-spitter in the whole wide world.
10   If they gave awards for this kind of thing, his room would be
11   covered in trophies. He is constantly spraying his saliva all
12   over my face, desk, and books. It's completely disgusting! I
13   might as well skip taking a shower in the mornings because
14   I know I'm going to get plenty wet when I come to his class!
15   I try to keep my head down so he doesn't get me straight in
16   the eye, but then I get in trouble for not paying attention. I
17   can't win!
18   One time he was extra close to my desk, and his spit
19   went straight into my mouth! My mouth! I thought I was
20   going to puke! Of course I had to tell my friends. It was
21   soooo gross! Want to know what my caring, compassionate
22   friends said? "Ewwww! It's like you kissed!" Then they told
23   everyone in class the next day. As if I would ever lock lips
24   with Mr. Sampson! Ick! He's *old!* And he spits, remember?
25   I think I am going to change my name. You can do that,
26   you know. Celebrities do it all the time. And I know exactly

1   what I'm going to be called: Zoe Zimmerman. That way I will
2   never be stuck in the front row again!

72. Ban on Soda

(Girl or Guy)

1   Juice is good. Juice is even pretty great. Juice is full of
2 vitamins and awesome sweetness. I have nothing *against*
3 juice. But I don't want it at every meal. Breakfast time?
4 Sure. Maybe even lunch time, if it's not orange juice. But
5 *dinnertime?* That's just not right.
6   My mom is on a juice kick. Or rather, she's on a "no
7 soda forever" kick. Which is actually a completely different
8 and more horrific thing. She refuses to buy soda anymore.
9 *No soda forever?* Who can live that way? How can *I* live that
10 way? I love that bubbly explosion in my mouth. It makes my
11 mouth come alive. Nothing comes close to that! Certainly
12 not smooth, flat juice! There's no tingly feeling. No burst of
13 flavor from all those wonderful little bubbles.
14   And what about the caffeine? How am I supposed to live
15 without that? How can I make it through long school days
16 and drama practice without a little extra push? How lively
17 can I be when I'm practically falling asleep on-stage? I *need*
18 my caffeine! I *need* my soda!
19   I think I've been pretty supportive up until now. When
20 she wanted to give up sweet treats, I supported her one
21 hundred percent. Even helped her clean out the cabinets
22 and throw all the cookies and hidden Halloween candy away.
23 To be honest, I prefer salty stuff anyway. When she took up
24 yoga, I even learned a few poses. And when she took up
25 running ... I ... well, I watched her run sometimes.
26   I feel like I've done everything I can to encourage her
27 healthy eating habits and lifestyle. But this is crossing the
28 line into insanity! Everyone needs something to indulge in.

1   Something that brings them joy. Something that bubbles in
2   their mouth! Come on, Mom! I need my soda!

73. My Mother the Weather Girl

(Girl or Guy)

1   Mrs. Obvious is what we should call my mother. I think
2 she is convinced it is her job to relay to us the most obvious
3 and random things she sees. It is so annoying. We walk out
4 the door, and it's, "Well, it's a beautiful sunshiny day
5 today." Gee, thanks Mom. Sure couldn't have seen that sun
6 shining all on my own. Or if we are coming out from a store
7 and it's starting to get dark, "It sure is getting late." Like
8 we can't tell time or something.

9   She is always saying quirky weather-related sayings too.
10 Like, "Red in the morning, sailor's warning. Red at night,
11 sailor's delight." What does that even mean? And why do I
12 care if a sailor is delighted or not? I swear my mother thinks
13 she's the up-and-coming weather girl for WKYX news.

14   When it's not nice out, we get, "Look at those clouds.
15 Looks like rain," or "Can you feel the humidity today?" No,
16 Mom. We can't see or feel or notice *anything* unless you tell
17 us! We can't see those gray clouds rolling in or that huge,
18 hot sun baking our backs unless you tell us all about it. We
19 can't think or observe for ourselves!

20   We need Mrs. Obvious to clue us in on *everything*. Like
21 the fact that tomorrow is July first, or that it's almost nine
22 o'clock, or that the wind "sure has picked up." Or what
23 every single person is doing on the television show that we
24 are watching. Why can't she just be quiet sometimes? Why
25 can't she keep the thought that pops into her head to
26 herself? Why can't she look out the window, see the

1 beautiful day, and *not* tell me about it? Why can she see
2 *everything else,* but she can't see that she's *driving me*
3 *crazy?*

74. Everyone Has Them!

(Girl)

1   I don't see what the big deal is. Girls have been getting
2 their ears pierced since my grandma was a teenager. Maybe
3 even before then. Why does it matter if I am twelve or
4 twenty? Isn't it my body? Shouldn't I be allowed to do what
5 I want to it? It's not like I'm asking for gauges or anything.
6 I just want simple little studs. Something to offset the fact
7 that I look like a boy! Is that too much to ask?

8   It's my mom's fault anyway. If she hadn't had the stylist
9 cut my hair so short, I might actually look like a girl. But
10 with this awful bob cut and *no* earrings, I can easily pass for
11 one of my brother's friends. Is she trying to scar me for life?
12 Because that's what's happening here. Wouldn't a couple of
13 earrings be better than years and years of therapy? Huh,
14 Mom?

15   Everyone in class has their ears pierced. All the girls, at
16 least. And even some of the boys! It's not like I'd be the only
17 one. It's not like I'd be the freak in class that everyone
18 would be staring at. No. That's me *now!* I'm the unisex kid
19 they call the he/she! OK, maybe they don't really call me
20 that. But they could!

21   All I'm asking for is two simple little holes in my ears.
22 Nothing major. Not even my cartilage. Definitely not my
23 nose or eyebrow or upper lip. Not my chin or belly button or
24 cheekbone. None of the weird places that people get
25 pierced. When you think about it, I could be asking for a
26 whole lot more. Something completely drastic and
27 unacceptable. I think I'm being pretty reasonable, don't
28 you? And I'll pay for it, too. I saved my birthday money.

1   Come on, Mom! All the moms let their daughters do this.
2   You want to be like all the other moms, don't you? *Don't*
3   *you?*

75. Bunk Beds Are for Babies

(Girl)

1   My friend Julie's bedroom is so cool. It is totally white
2   and black with red accents that just pop out at you. Like a
3   red heart-shaped pillow on her bed. Or a red lampshade. Or
4   a red throw blanket. For the black and white part, she's got
5   different pictures from cool places like France, Italy, and
6   Greece. Her clock looks like the Eiffel Tower. Her whole
7   room is soooo sophisticated.

8   Want to know what I have in my room? Wallpaper with
9   picket fences, flowers, and ladybugs. Yes, that's right.
10   Ladybugs. I have a rainbow lampshade and clouds painted
11   on my ceiling. And if that's not bad enough, there is a shelf
12   full of every stuffed ladybug ever sold right above my closet
13   doors. The same closet doors that have vines painted all
14   over them. Like I live in a garden or something.

15   Perfect for a girl my age, right? Of course not. It's perfect
16   for my six-year-old sister, who I share a room with. That's
17   fair, right? Of course not. Isn't it time I got a room of my
18   own? I want a room that is free and clear of cutesy bugs and
19   painted grass. I want a room that absolutely doesn't have
20   any type of flower in it. I want a room that doesn't look like
21   a preschool room!

22   Do you have any idea how embarrassing it is to have
23   friends over? It's like we've gone back in time to
24   kindergarten. I feel like I should offer them finger paints or
25   something! All I want is a room like Julie's. A room I can be
26   proud of. A room I can relax in and not have to hear my

1 sister's sing-along songs.
2   Haven't I paid my dues long enough? Haven't I lived in
3 this picket-fence prison way beyond a normal sentence?
4 Can't you set me free? Can't you *please* set me free?

76. My Phone Is Driving Me Crazy

(Girl or Guy)

1   I may just throw my phone across the room. Or maybe
2 flush it down the toilet. Or maybe as a car drives by, I will
3 pitch it under the tires. Or maybe I could drop it off a really
4 tall cliff. Or off a bridge. Do you think the insurance on the
5 phone will cover that? Because I can't keep this phone one
6 minute longer! It's driving me crazy.
7   Buzz. Buzz. Buzz. Do you hear that? Sounds like a huge
8 bumblebee, doesn't it? It's annoying, isn't it? Well, it isn't a
9 cute little insect, it's my phone! It's been going crazy!
10 Buzz. Buzz. Buzz. That's what it does all day long. It
11 just randomly buzzes like I'm getting a ton of text messages
12 or emails. Then when I check it ... nothing! Not one thing to
13 make it vibrate like that. I think it's possessed or
14 something. Like some kind of evil spirit has invaded my
15 phone, and it's slowly torturing me!
16 It's so embarrassing, because I never know when it's
17 going to happen. So I'll be sitting in class, and buzz, buzz,
18 buzz. There it goes. Switching back and forth from vibrate
19 mode all on its own. So when I think it's on vibrate, it's
20 actually got the sound on! Which means when I actually *do*
21 get a text, it pings really loudly and gets me in trouble! The
22 teacher will say, "Put that on silent!" Like duh! I'm trying
23 to! How do I tell her that it has a mind of its own? She'll
24 think I'm crazy.
25 I would almost rather *not* have a phone than have to put
26 up with this any longer. I've begged Mom to get me a new
27 one, but she won't do it until I'm eligible for an upgrade.
28 That's six more months! I can't take this kind of torture for
29 *six more months!*

77. Dad's the Jockey, Not Me

(Girl or Guy)

1   So I know it's every kid's dream to own a horse. All little
2 kids use broomsticks and such and ride around their
3 houses and pretend they are riding a stallion or a
4 thoroughbred. Heck, I probably did that too. But that didn't
5 mean I *actually* wanted to own a horse. If that were the
6 case, then when I made a spaceship out of cardboard, I
7 really wanted a spaceship too. OK. Scratch that. Because I
8 probably *did* want both of those things when I was little. But
9 now I'm older, and I definitely do *not* want a horse. Or a
10 spaceship, for that matter.

11   But here I am with a beautiful black stallion munching
12 grass out in our backyard, and I have no idea how to tell my
13 dad that I'm completely terrified of it! It's huge! And it's tall,
14 and it snorts at me. And when I sit on it, I feel like I'm a
15 million miles from the ground. I know if I fall off, I'm going
16 to break every bone in my body.

17   I don't want to seem ungrateful. I'm sure horses are *not*
18 cheap. And my dad was so happy to give it to me. He's been
19 a jockey all his life. He lives, eats, and breathes horses.
20 Wait ... scratch that. Ha ha. He definitely does *not* eat
21 horses! But he is seriously obsessed with them! And he
22 wants me to be the same way. He *expects* me to be the
23 same way. In fact, if I wasn't growing so tall, he'd be
24 training me as a jockey already! Thank goodness I got my
25 height from my mom.

1   I actually do love horses from a distance. They're really
2 gorgeous animals. So graceful. Not scary at all ... when they
3 are across the field. I love taking pictures of them and even
4 drawing them. I just don't like riding them!
5   So how do I tell my dad that even though most kids in
6 the world would kill to have a horse, I would be much
7 happier without one? It's going to break his little jockey
8 heart!

78. My Dad Looks Like an Ape

(Girl or Guy)

1   I love doing all kinds of things with my dad. We hike,
2 bike, play basketball, and even jog together. He's very
3 active and in great shape. He's a ton of fun too, so I'm glad
4 that we get to hang out a lot. At least, I'm glad nine months
5 out of the year. The summer months ... not so much.

6   I feel bad to even admit this, but being with my dad at
7 the pool is embarrassing! He looks like an ape! He's got so
8 much back hair that you can't even see his skin! He doesn't
9 even have to wear sunscreen because the hair blocks out
10 the sun! It looks like he's wearing a woolly sweater!

11   And it's not just his back. He's got hair everywhere!
12 Chest hair. Neck hair. Ear hair. And the normal places too,
13 which are extra hairy — arm hair, leg hair, and underarm
14 hair that I swear could be braided. The only places he
15 doesn't have hair is the palms of his hands and the bottom
16 of his feet! The man is like Sasquatch! In fact, I've heard
17 people whispering things about him.

18   I wish I just didn't care, because I wouldn't hurt my
19 dad's feelings for the world. But it's hard not to notice
20 everyone staring at him. And sometimes they point, too. So
21 far I don't think he's noticed. But just in case, I feel like I
22 have to do something! Maybe I could get him a spa day for
23 Father's Day this year that includes a waxing! I'm sure
24 they'll charge double when they see him, but I'm willing to
25 use all the money I've saved to get it done. I just hope
26 they've got some heavy-duty wax strips, because I think it's
27 going to take a whole lot to get all that hair off!

79. We'll Keep in Touch

(Girl)

1   My best friend Heather is moving to California on Friday.
2 That's on the complete opposite side of the United States! It
3 might as well be China. We will never be able to see each
4 other ever again. It's so unfair that her parents are taking her
5 away from me. Don't they know we're practically sisters? How
6 can her dad's company do this to them? To us?

7   We've been friends since kindergarten. She's been at my
8 house or I've been at her house almost every weekend since
9 we've been old enough to have sleepovers. I even call her
10 parents "Mom" and "Dad." Or I did until this happened. Now
11 I don't ever want to speak to them. They didn't even ask her
12 if they could move! How could they do that? Not even give her
13 the choice! They can't just rip her away from here!

14   Why can't they just let her stay here with me? I *know*
15 my parents would take her. They can see how miserable
16 we've been since they told us the news. What's one more
17 mouth to feed? My brother could just cut back a little,
18 because he eats too much anyway! And her parents could
19 come visit her during the holidays! It's a win-win situation!

20   OK, maybe not win-win. But her moving away is *lose-*
21 *lose!* And I don't want to lose my best friend! Oh, we've
22 promised to keep in touch — text, Skype, email, Facebook,
23 Twitter, talk on the phone — the works. But let's be real.
24 How long will that last? We all know how that goes. Before
25 long we'll move on, and our friendship will be a distant
26 memory ... although ... with today's technology ... maybe we
27 really *will* stay friends forever! I mean, it's possible, right?

80. I Am Not a Jinx

(Girl)

1 There is a black cloud hanging over my head, and
2 everyone in school can see it. They've started calling me
3 "the jinx," and they point and snicker at me when I walk
4 down the hall. I've been getting mean notes shoved in my
5 locker threatening me if I attend the school basketball
6 games!

7 But how can I not attend? My boyfriend is the star player
8 on the team! At least he *was* the star player ... until I
9 became his girlfriend. Now he can't seem to make a basket
10 to save his life! And everyone's blaming me! We haven't won
11 a game ever since we became a couple, and we were
12 undefeated before then.

13 When they aren't calling me a jinx, they say it's because
14 I'm distracting him! When I'm not doing anything! I don't
15 even cheer for him so that they can't say that about me! It's
16 like I can't win no matter what. They love making me the
17 scapegoat for the team playing badly! Because it's not just
18 Barry whose game is off now — it's the whole team! Well,
19 they can't pin that on me! I'm not going out with the whole
20 team!

21 I think Barry and I are going to stage a fake breakup so
22 that everyone will get off my back. Then when the team
23 starts winning again, we'll come clean and tell everyone
24 we're still together! That will show them all that I am *not* a
25 jinx! Of course for that plan to work, they have to really
26 start winning ... otherwise, maybe it really is me!

81. Locker Buddies — Not!

(Girl)

1   My friend is a slob. Which would be OK if she only kept
2   her room that way. But the problem is not just hers now,
3   it's mine. See, we're locker buddies. And I use the term
4   "buddies" loosely at this moment, because I actually am to
5   the point where I loathe her. I loathe her cracker crumbs all
6   over my books. I loathe her smelly gym socks stuffed in the
7   back corner of the locker. I loathe her hairbrush full of hair
8   hanging from the hook at the top. And I really loathe the
9   papers she crumples up and throws on top of everything.

10   Has she never heard of a trash can? I even bought a mini
11   garbage can for the locker. See this? Completely empty. She
12   refuses to actually use it! It takes only a second more to
13   shove her trash in here. But no! She'd rather clutter up the
14   locker. Last week she left a banana peel in here for two
15   days. Well, actually *she* would've left it in here forever. *I'm*
16   the one who took it and threw it away!

17   How do I tell her that I'm not her maid or her mother?
18   She needs to pick up after herself and keep things
19   organized! It's just rude to keep things like this when
20   there's another person involved! I can't even find my books
21   half the time! I've been late for class just because I have to
22   dig my stuff out of this black hole of a locker. There are
23   some things I think are lost forever!

24   Now she's saying how she wants us to room together in
25   college! Is she crazy? I don't care if that is years away, I
26   wouldn't live with her for all the money in the world! I'd need
27   therapy to deal with all that clutter and nastiness! But how
28   do I tell her that not only do I *not* want to be her roommate,
29   I want her to move *out* of my locker?

82. They're Not Your Friends

(Girl)

1   It's getting to the point that I don't even want to have
2 my friends come to my house anymore. My mom thinks that
3 *my* friends are *her* friends. Every time they come over, she's
4 right there, chatting them up, telling them stories, giving
5 them advice, telling jokes. It's like she's reliving her
6 younger years with *my* friends!

7   I tried talking to her about it. I even did it nicely. Told
8 her that she didn't *have* to feel obligated to entertain my
9 friends. That I appreciated her making them feel welcome,
10 but she really didn't have to hang with us so long. I guess I
11 was too nice, though, because she didn't take the hint at
12 all. In fact, her exact words were, "It's no problem at all. I
13 think they really like me!"

14   The real problem is … I think she's right. They *do* like
15 her. They think she's cool and funny and nothing at all like
16 their own moms. I think they actually *like* her hanging out
17 with us. So no problem, right? Wrong. Now I'm not sure if
18 my friends come to hang out with *me* or to hang out with
19 my *mom!* To be honest, I'm pretty sure that they actually
20 like her more than me. That's pathetic, huh? That I'm
21 jealous of my own mom!

22   Why does my mom have to be the young, cool one? Why
23 can't she be like Sandi's mom who has gray hair and knits?
24 No one ever wants to hang around her! Or even Jenna's
25 mom who is always working and never home! We've barely
26 even laid eyes on her in all the years we've been friends.

1 How perfect would that be? She could even be like Tessa's
2 mom! She's good about taking us to the mall or movies and
3 stuff, but then she *leaves,* like normal moms do! She
4 doesn't invite herself along and then sit in the middle of us
5 and hog the conversation! I guess I'm just going to have to
6 set my mom straight. My friends are *not* her friends!

83. Clearly I Am Not the Karate Kid

(Girl or Guy)

1 I have always wanted to take karate. Probably ever since
2 I saw a bunch of Jackie Chan movies when I was little. He
3 is so cool. And he makes it look so easy! The way he flies
4 through the air, knocking people out with such grace. I
5 swear he stays suspended in midair for minutes at a time!
6   I knew I would never be as good as Jackie. I mean, who
7 can be, right? But I figured I could at least learn some of the
8 cool moves he did. Boy, was I wrong. Karate is hard.
9 Especially for someone like me who can't really walk, talk,
10 and chew gum at the same time. At least that's what my
11 friends say about me. To be honest, they're one hundred
12 percent right! I am the klutziest person there ever was!
13   When I start kicking in class, I look like a maniac. There
14 is *zero* grace coming out of this body, I tell you. I probably
15 look like a freakish bucking bronco! Half the time I can't get
16 my arms and legs to move at the same time. It's like *one* or
17 the *other!* How am I supposed to concentrate on swinging
18 my arms when I have to concentrate on when to kick my
19 legs? It's like you have to be a genius or something. You
20 know how they have that test where you pat your head and
21 rub your stomach at the same time? Well, I can't do it!
22   I'm always tripping over my uniform belt. Why do they
23 have to make the darn thing so long, anyway? Do you know
24 how embarrassing it is to stumble across the mat and dive
25 into someone because you can't do a leap kick without
26 getting tangled in your own belt?
27   I guess the lesson learned here is this: I will never be
28 Jackie Chan. In fact, I will never even come close to being
29 the dirt on Jackie Chan's shoe.

84. Ours Is Just as Good

(Girl)

1   I really don't get why Jessica didn't invite my friend
2 Casey and me to her slumber party tonight. She invited
3 almost every single girl in the seventh grade class! Why
4 would she exclude us? Casey and I are tons of fun. We're
5 always cracking each other up. In fact, I would call us the
6 life of any party! One time, I almost peed my pants from
7 laughing so hard at something Casey and I did. That's just
8 the way it is with us. *Hilarious!* We make everything fun. So
9 I really don't understand why we didn't make the cut
10 tonight. Even bug-eyed Allison got invited, and I heard she
11 still pees the bed sometimes! Who wants to risk that?

12   Well, when Jessica's party is boring and stupid and her
13 bed is wet with Allison's pee, she'll regret not inviting us.
14 Especially when she finds out that I'm having my *own*
15 slumber party tonight, and I didn't invite her! That's right.
16 Two can play at that game!

17   And who cares if it's only Casey and me? We'll have a
18 blast anyway. I've got lots of snacks and games and movies.
19 I even made Oreo balls for dessert! I bet Jessica would
20 regret missing out on those because they are like little
21 pieces of heaven, I tell you! They just melt in your mouth. I
22 bet her snacks aren't even close to being as yummy as
23 mine!

24   Mom says we can stay up as late as we want, too. I bet
25 Jessica's mom didn't say that. They probably have an early
26 bedtime. Like lights out at ten o'clock or something awful
27 like that. And they probably can't eat in their basement like
28 we can. Who knows? Jessica probably doesn't even have a

1   basement! She's probably got all those girls crammed into
2   some tiny bedroom where they have to all sleep on the floor
3   or draw straws for the tiny little bed!
4   My sleepover is soooo much better than that! Now that
5   I think about it, I'm *glad* I didn't get invited to stupid
6   Jessica's party. It doesn't sound fun at all!

85. Cheers and Tears

(Girl)

1   It was so exciting hearing the coach call out my name
2   when she read the list of who made the cheerleading team.
3   My heart was pounding in my ears so loudly that I barely
4   heard my name being called. I was so nervous! But when it
5   sank in that she really did say my name, I couldn't help but
6   let out a little squeal of excitement! I'd been waiting for this
7   moment since elementary school. I knew that making the
8   middle school team was just the stepping stone I needed to
9   make the high school team in a few years!

10   So I guess you could say I was pretty focused on hearing
11   *my* name, which is why it didn't dawn on me right away that
12   I didn't hear my best friend Kara's name. But when I turned
13   to hug her over my good news, I knew from her face that her
14   name had not been called. My stomach sank. This wasn't
15   how it was supposed to happen. The plan always was that
16   we would make the squad together. I stopped my hug with
17   my arms mid-air and let them drop to my sides.

18   "It's OK," she said with tears in her eyes. We both knew
19   it wasn't.

20   My mind raced as I tried to think of something to say. I
21   knew she was devastated. I was too. It wouldn't be the
22   same without her. But was I supposed to quit the team
23   before I even started just because she didn't make it? Did
24   she expect that of me? Because I really didn't want to. Did
25   that make me a bad friend? Was I supposed to sacrifice my
26   spot on the team for her? Would she do the same for me?
27   Would I expect her to? Or would I be happy for her? Wouldn't
28   I want her to still do it anyway? Even if I was the one who

1 didn't make it?
2   I decided I would. Of course it was easy to decide that
3 given the circumstances. Still, I believed if the roles were
4 reversed, that is exactly what I would do. I would be
5 gracious. I would congratulate her. I would be happy for her
6 ... OK, maybe not happy ... but I wouldn't take it away from
7 her. I had to believe she'd do the same for me.
8   "You're going to be great," she said, and I exhaled the
9 breath I didn't even know I was holding. I was right. Kara
10 *would* do the same for me.

86. I Am Not Wearing That

(Girl)

1   I don't mind that my mother is sentimental. In fact, it's
2 been kind of nice over the years to flip back through boxes
3 and boxes of old memories of mine. The woman literally
4 keeps everything I do. Papers from kindergarten.
5 Homemade ornaments. Ribbons. Preschool drawings. Even
6 doodlings on napkins or paper menus. It's crazy. But
7 awesome, too, because I can practically relive my whole
8 childhood by going through those boxes.
9   She has boxes and boxes of my old baby clothes, too.
10 Do you know how weird it is to look at something so tiny
11 and know that you used to fit in it? Cute little bootie shoes
12 and tiny onesies that look too small for even a doll to fit in!
13   Not to mention the boatloads of pictures the woman has
14 of me! You would think I was a celebrity or something. I
15 swear she didn't miss a milestone. Actually, I don't think
16 she's missed one smile. The woman is camera crazy! But
17 again, it's pretty cool seeing how I've grown from such a
18 plump blob of a baby to a teenage girl!
19   The problem isn't with all the stuff of *mine* she's kept.
20 It's that she's kept all the same things of *hers.* Every card,
21 ticket stub, pressed flower, award, etc! And every single
22 fancy dress she's ever worn, which wouldn't be a problem at
23 all, except she wants *me* to start wearing them! I'm serious!
24 She wants me to wear the same dress that she wore to *her*
25 eighth-grade dance to *my* eighth-grade dance. I'm sure you
26 can only imagine how different the style is between then and
27 now! And if you can't imagine, let me just give you a hint:
28 her dress has *shoulder pads!* And *lace!* I cannot be seen in

1 a dress with shoulder pads and lace!
2   Which is why I'm faking sick right now. It's the only
3 thing I could do! But I don't want to miss *all* my upcoming
4 dances, even though I don't see how I'm ever going to go!
5 Next year's dress involves a hoop skirt! I am definitely not
6 going to freshman prom in a hoop skirt!
7   Do you think there's a way to breed moths? Or termites?
8 Or maybe find a dress-eating goat?

87. Our Family Tree Has a Bunch of Twigs

(Girl or Guy)

1   My father is obsessed with figuring out our family tree.
2   He spends hours and hours scouring the Internet for
3   information about when my family came to America and
4   who married who and all that stuff that no one really cares
5   about. I mean, does it really matter if my great-great-great
6   grandfather came over on the Mayflower or not? Who knows
7   if half the stuff you find is even true or not? I seriously doubt
8   it is because those sites know that you can't really verify
9   what they're saying. They can make all the fake documents
10 they want because who could possibly know the difference?
11   I don't even know why my dad wants to know more
12 about our family. The people we see all the time are
13 interesting enough that you don't need to go back hundreds
14 of years! Take Uncle Charlie, for instance. The dude is *nuts.*
15 He is fifty years old and still dresses up in costumes to go
16 to the comic book store when a new issue comes out. Just
17 so they'll give him a free copy of the latest episode! Who
18 does that?
19   Or what about my cousin Gina? She has a full body
20 tattoo! *Full body!* Even on her face! She looks like she could
21 work for the circus! Or there's always my Aunt Betty. She
22 has been married five times already, and she's only in her
23 thirties. It takes a whole branch to chart her part of the
24 family tree alone. And Mom says the guys she marries
25 aren't anything but a bunch of twigs anyway. Ha, ha!
26   But if that's not enough to convince you, take my cousin
27 Harold. He lost his arm to a shark. For real. Got it ripped

1 right off. And survived! Tell me *that's* not way more
2 interesting than what country we may or may not have
3 emigrated from! Dad needs to quit worrying about the family
4 tree and write a family novel instead!

88. Swim Trunks Should Always Fit

(Guy)

1   Here is a very important life lesson for you. *Always,* and
2 I do mean *always,* make sure that when you buy your swim
3 trunks, you *make sure they fit.* In fact, you may want to err
4 on the side of caution and buy them a size or two smaller.
5 You definitely do *not* want to get them a size *too big.* Saggy
6 bottoms may be OK in how you wear your pants, but trust
7 me, it is *not* how you want to wear your trunks.
8   Just ask anyone who was at the pool on Saturday and
9 saw my swim trunks floating in the pool! It was so
10 humiliating! There I was performing the most perfect dive
11 from the top board, one I had practiced hundreds of times
12 and couldn't wait to show everyone. I knew it was going to
13 be great. That's why I made sure that *all* my friends were
14 paying attention to me when I went up to the board. Big
15 mistake, right?
16   I split the water with my hands perfectly. Felt the water
17 glide over me smoothly and then whoosh! There went my
18 bathing suit! Not just to my ankles, but right off the legs!
19   I didn't know what to do! How do you gracefully recover
20 from something like that? There was no place to hide! Water
21 is see-through, in case you didn't know! So everyone could
22 see *everything* about me! The moments it took to get my
23 trunks back on seemed like an eternity. I could hear
24 everyone laughing and see them pointing. I couldn't get out
25 of the pool and into the locker room fast enough.
26   So believe me when I tell you, this is a life lesson you do
27 not want to have to learn on your own.

89. Dear Me

(Girl)

1 Dear Leah,
2   If you are reading this now, then it means you have
3 reached the ripe old age of twenty-five! I guess that means
4 you have already had all the fun you're ever going to have!
5 Ha, ha! You're probably married and on your way to the five
6 kids I always said I would have.
7   It's so weird to think of myself reading this letter that I
8 wrote to myself at age eleven. It's kind of mind-blowing,
9 actually. I'm supposed to remind you of the little girl you
10 were back in middle school. All the hopes and dreams I had
11 for our life.
12   Did you become a physician's assistant like you wanted
13 to be? Did you find the kind of guy who would love the
14 outdoors as much as you do? Did you have the big dream
15 wedding on a beach that you made a scrapbook about? Did
16 you go to New York City to live for a few months after
17 graduation? Did you study abroad?
18   Did you graduate as valedictorian? Did you make lots of
19 friends in high school and go on a really cool spring break
20 trip your senior year? Did you keep in touch with your best
21 friend April? Please say you did! We've promised to be
22 friends forever!
23   I hope that reading this letter reminds you that I had a
24 plan for my life. A great and wonderful plan to live a full life,
25 to help people, and to fall in love deeply. If you haven't had
26 a chance to do all the things I've dreamed about ... make
27 time now! It's not too late! You're only twenty-five!

90. Not Your Nosy Neighbor

(Girl or Guy)

1   I'm not one to point the finger at someone, especially
2   when it comes to being messy. You should see my room. I
3   pretty much live like a pig. Just ask my mom. She nags me,
4   like, every single day, even though my room shouldn't
5   bother her at all ... it's *my* room. But I have to say that even
6   me, a self-proclaimed pig, is disgusted by my neighbor's
7   house.

8   Mr. Harris is a hoarder. Pure and simple. He has so
9   much junk around his house that it looks like a yard sale is
10 going on there twenty-four-seven. People have even stopped
11 by to ask him how much he wants for something. But of
12 course he never sells. He won't part with a single piece of
13 junk he has lying around. He's got car parts, old televisions,
14 appliances, used tires ... everything! You name it and he's
15 got it!

16 My parents have tried to be understanding, which I
17 *know* must be killing my mom, as upset as she gets with
18 me over my messy room. They say that he's got a problem
19 and that we should try to understand. But I think their
20 patience is wearing thin. Mom just spent a fortune on these
21 tall bushes to plant in the front yard between our house and
22 his. Then she got someone to come quote a price for
23 installing a privacy fence in the backyard. The most
24 surprising part is that she said "Do it" even though the
25 fence is going to cost a *ton* of money. She even used the
26 money in her Hawaii vacation fund to help pay for it. Believe
27 me, that means *desperate!* Mom never touches that money!

1   When I suggested we just move, I thought my mom was
2   going to cry. She asked me who would ever consider buying
3   a house next to that junkyard, and then she said I should
4   just move in with Mr. Harris since I live just like him! I have
5   to say, that hit home pretty hard! I spent the next two days
6   cleaning up my room — the last thing I want is to become
a weird old hoarder!

91. I Am Old Enough to Walk Home with My Friends

(Girl or Guy)

1   I am so tired of my mother treating me like a baby. She
2   has so many rules and this weird paranoia about what could
3   happen to me. I feel like I'm living in a bubble. I just now
4   got her to agree to let me walk home from school with my
5   friends. *Just now!* I'm twelve years old. Almost a teenager,
6   and my mom is making such a big deal out of it!

7   I know kids who have been walking home *alone* since
8   kindergarten! Most of my friends have been latchkey kids
9   since third grade! But not me. My mom hasn't worked since
10 I was born, so she is at the house *every day* after school.
11 She hasn't missed picking me up one time since I started
12 school. Not even when she was sick!

13 So I guess it is a big win that I finally got her to agree
14 to let me walk home and *not* have her pick me up. But you'd
15 think we lived in the world's highest crime area the way she
16 is carrying on. She's drilled me over and over about what to
17 do if I get out of school and my friends aren't there to walk
18 with me. She even got me a cell phone so I can call her. I
19 am absolutely *not* to walk home alone. She practically made
20 me sign a contract about it.

21 The big day finally came, and I was halfway to the house
22 when I saw her ... she was actually tailing me! Following us
23 from school to the house. I couldn't believe it! I tried not to
24 keep looking back at her, because I didn't want my friends
25 to know. Do you have any idea how mortifying that would
26 be? Your mother stalking you as you walk home from
27 school? I don't know how she's ever going to let me go to
28 high school, much less college! She is seriously going to
29 need some therapy.

92. Believe Me,
I've Been Punished Enough

(Girl or Guy)

1   I know it was the wrong thing to do. I knew it when I did
2   it that it was the wrong thing to do. And I *truly* regret doing
3   it. *Far* more than my parents could *ever* know. I regret it way
4   more than any kind of punishment they could give me to try
5   and *make* me regret it ... but they don't believe me. They
6   think I was out carousing the night away with my friends
7   and that I need to be grounded for the rest of my life!

8   But that wasn't the case at all. I *was* out of the house
9   without permission. Yeah, I snuck out the window. But it
10   was *not* the fun I thought it was going to be. See, my friends
11   wanted to hang out at the cemetery down the street at
12   midnight to prove that we weren't scared. It sounded cool at
13   the time. Playing hide and seek behind the gravestones,
14   reading the headstones, and making up stories on how they
15   died, maybe even performing a séance or something.

16   Let me just tell you, it wasn't cool at all. In fact, it was
17   *terrifying!* Do you have any idea how creepy a graveyard is
18   when it's pitch-black outside, and the moon is barely
19   shining? Every little breeze on my skin felt like someone
20   running their cold, bony ghost fingers over my body! I can't
21   even guess how many times I almost screamed out loud! I
22   was shaking, I was so scared. I couldn't wait to get back
23   home.

24   In fact, that's why I got caught. I practically threw
25   myself through my window to get back into the house, and
26   I landed with a huge thump. That's when my parents came

1 running and found me fully dressed on the floor beside my
2 window. It didn't take long to realize I had not been in my
3 bed like they'd thought.
4   I guess the grounding won't be so bad, though. At least
5 I have an excuse for not going back out with my friends.
6 They're talking about doing it again ... maybe even camping
7 out there! I definitely will *not* miss being a part of that. In
8 fact, I may keep getting in trouble to make sure I *stay*
9 grounded!

93. Kicked Off the Team

(Guy)

1   I guess there's no hiding it anymore. I've done a pretty
2 good job keeping it a secret all week, but tonight at the
3 game, my dad is going to find out that I've been benched
4 from the team. I know I should've told him before now. Then
5 he might not have even bothered to come. Why would he? I
6 won't be playing. He wouldn't have wasted his time or his
7 money. But I just couldn't find the perfect time to tell him.
8   He's obsessed with football. He's been throwing the
9 pigskin around with me since I could barely walk. Mom says
10 he had a football and a jersey waiting for me the day I was
11 born. He has never missed a game of mine. I think he's so
12 proud of me playing because he never could. His family was
13 always moving around so much that he never got a chance
14 to prove himself. Never got a chance to pay his dues. So
15 how could I tell him that I got benched? Especially *why* I got
16 benched!
17   I didn't realize that my grades were slipping so low.
18 Sure, I missed turning in a couple of homework
19 assignments, but I didn't think it was a big deal. And then
20 I forgot about this huge test in science last Friday. Like
21 *completely* forgot about it. So I knew I'd failed it. Grade
22 updates come out on Mondays for the coaches. That's when
23 I got pulled into the office and told I was suspended from
24 the team until my grades improve. Suspended!
25   My dad is going to flip! He doesn't understand making
26 mistakes. Especially if it impacts football in any way. But
27 maybe he doesn't have to know ... maybe he'll just think
28 that coach isn't playing me tonight! That could work! Maybe

1   I could even fake an injury … I could limp when I walk to the
2   bench … That's it! And then next week I'll get my grades
3   up!

94. They Met Online

(Girl or Guy)

1   I don't mind that my dad has a girlfriend. I really don't.
2 It keeps him busy and out of my hair and actually keeps him
3 in a much better mood than when he was single. He sure
4 was grumpy then!

5   What I *do* mind is *how* my dad got a girlfriend. It's so
6 embarrassing. It's almost as bad as those rich old men who
7 get a mail-order bride. I mean, only desperate people join
8 online dating sites, right? Not a nice good-looking guy like
9 my dad. He's got a great personality, too. Shouldn't he have
10 met someone the right way? The old-fashioned way? Like
11 while walking our dog at the park? Or while squeezing
12 cantaloupes at the grocery store? Or maybe standing in line
13 at the post office?

14   I hate it when we're all out together and he and Andrea
15 tell people they met online. Don't they realize how pathetic
16 that sounds? Like, "Hey, we don't have any social skills to
17 meet someone face to face. We had to do it online like
18 creepy people."

19   Who even knows if half the stuff about her is true? Sure,
20 she seems like she's on the up and up. But how do we really
21 know? And what if she only went after my dad for his
22 money? I'm sure it made him a whole lot more attractive
23 when she saw that M.D. after his last name! That's just one
24 of those things that you aren't advertising when you meet
25 someone by chance at the grocery store or library! They
26 don't get your resume right off the bat! They actually have
27 to want to get to know you first. I just wonder if Andrea
28 would've even noticed my dad out in public. Makes you

1   wonder, doesn't it?
2   All I know is, when I'm old enough to fall in love, I'm
3   doing it the right way!

95. What a Faker!

(Girl or Guy)

1   I wonder if my mom will believe me this time. I know I
2 joke around with her a lot ... always teasing her and
3 pretending that I am hurt. I like to do that to Mom. She gets
4 so upset thinking I am hurt, and then I spring it on her —
5 I'm just faking! It's really funny, even though she doesn't
6 think so. But this time I think I really am hurt.

7   You see, I was riding my bike on my way home from the
8 city pool, where I had a great time with all my friends. I was
9 looking forward to getting home for some lunch. I was
10 thinking to myself that life just could not be any better than
11 this moment. No school for three months, and all I had to
12 do was enjoy my summer. What a life!

13   And then it happened. The wet towel that I had wrapped
14 around the front handle bars slipped off and tangled up in
15 the spokes of the tire! Before I could stop, the front wheel
16 locked up and over the handle bars I flew! All I could
17 remember was hitting the pavement and the bike toppling
18 over me. And then it occurred to me. I really was hurt this
19 time. My shoulder was killing me, and I felt faint. It was a
20 good thing that I was only a block away from my house,
21 because I was in no shape to ride the bike home.

22   As I walked toward my house, I began to see stars! I
23 knew something was wrong. I could not move my arm.
24 When I walked into the house, my mom was on the phone.
25 I wondered if I would be able to convince her that I really
26 was hurt. Especially after all the times I pretended to be in
27 pain just as a joke.

28   But I must have looked worse than I thought. "Mom," I
29 said. She turned around and before I could even say another

1   word my mom's face had a shocked look and she hung up
2   the phone immediately. I don't even think she said good-
3   bye! I guess even with all the fake-outs, my mom knows me
4   better than I thought!

96. What a Chicken!

(Girl or Guy)

1 My sister is ruining everything! My parents had this
2 great tropical vacation all planned out for us. I'm talking
3 amazing blue water and palm trees like you only see on
4 postcards. It was going to be amazing. Beyond amazing!
5 It's the kind of vacation that you dream about taking.
6 Maybe even plan as your honeymoon. A once-in-a-lifetime
7 opportunity that you would remember for the rest of your
8 life. We were even going to go swimming with the dolphins.
9 And maybe even with the stingrays! How cool would that be
10 to swim with creatures that you usually only see on
11 television! Dad even said he might go down in the cage and
12 see the sharks. The sharks! I don't think I could've handled
13 that, but I would've loved to hear all about it from my dad!
14   Anyway, that's when our dream vacation got flushed
15 down the toilet. My little sister heard the word "shark" and
16 started freaking out. She was totally fine about the vacation
17 before then. Couldn't wait to snorkel in the clear blue ocean.
18 But breathe the word "shark," and she's crying like a
19 lunatic. Well, where did she think sharks live? Doesn't she
20 know that the possibility of getting attacked by a shark is
21 probably less likely than getting struck by lightning? And
22 yet I still see her walking around outside!
23   I say we still go and she can sit out on the beach and
24 wave to us. But Mom and Dad say it isn't fair to go on a
25 vacation where we *all* aren't happy. I agree. Leave her at
26 Grandma's house then, and she won't have to *go* on a
27 vacation where she isn't happy. It's so ridiculous. Because
28 of her stupid paranoia, we all have to suffer. Can't they just

1   get her some therapy between now and then?
2   Want to know where my parents are planning to take us
3   now? The Grand Canyon. A big, stupid hole in the ground!
4   Maybe I need to come up with some irrational fear that will
5   keep us from going *there!*

97. Turtle Racing

(Girl or Guy)

1   My brother has come up with a new form of
2   entertainment with his friends. However, just so you know,
3   I use the term "entertainment" loosely, because I certainly
4   don't see anything fun in what they're doing. In fact, I
5   almost fell asleep the last time. Want to know what my
6   genius brother's newest obsession is? Turtle racing. That's
7   right. *Turtles.* And *racing.* They don't really go together, do
8   they?

9   What kind of morons actually think that could be fun?
10 My brother and his friends, I guess. They even made a
11 racecourse for the tiny creatures and painted numbers on
12 their shells. As if they were going to be flying by so fast,
13 they wouldn't be able to keep track of them. It's ridiculous.
14 I honestly think that it would be more fun to watch paint
15 dry!

16 They even video the races and then upload them to the
17 Internet. Who would watch such boring stuff? But they have
18 one video that's actually had over five hundred views! I can't
19 believe that *five hundred* stupid people actually watched the
20 most boring race of the century. I swear they move like an
21 inch an hour! Most of the time you think they might have
22 died on the track!

23 Now they're trying to get me to buy a turtle too. They
24 want more competition. Apparently it just isn't fun enough
25 with only the five turtles they have between them. Well, I'm
26 not buying. I've got better things to do with my money and
27 my time than to waste it watching turtles move like
28 molasses. You'd think they would have at least tried frogs.

1   Or beetles. Or something that actually *moves* every once in
2   a while!
3   Well, Mr. Life-of-the-Party, I hate to break it to you, but
4   you can count me out! Turtle racing just isn't my thing!

98. What Did I Do?

(Girl or Guy)

1   For the first time in my life, I'm sitting in the principal's
2   office, and it was not my fault! This is so embarrassing, and
3   I am going to be in some serious trouble when I get home.
4   I hardly even know what the principal looks like, and in a few
5   minutes, he'll be giving me the "third degree." Surely when
6   he sees me, he'll know I am a good kid. Maybe he will look
7   up my grades and notice that I make the honor roll almost
8   every quarter. I can't believe I am in this predicament.

9   It happened at the end of last period. I play the bass
10 drum in band class, and mean Mr. Hughes gave us a new
11 piece of music to practice. I like playing in the drum section
12 because I get to be in the back of the classroom with my
13 two best friends. I try to pay attention and not goof around
14 much with my buddies. As soon as Mr. Hughes gave us the
15 new sheet music, I knew I would have trouble learning my
16 part. After all, Mr. Hughes is strict, and he never gives me
17 much individual help.

18 So there I was in the back of the room, standing with
19 my big bass drum. Mr. Hughes walked to the front of the
20 room and raised his baton to begin the new piece. As the
21 song began, I thought I was doing pretty well, and then all
22 of a sudden Mr. Hughes stopped the band. And you will
23 never guess what he did! He started staring me down like I
24 did something wrong! I know I am not a great band student,
25 but why would he be singling me out? And the worst thing
26 is that he didn't say a thing. He just kept staring at me!

27 Then guess what happened next. The first row of flutes
28 turned around to see who Mr. Hughes was staring down.

1 How embarrassing! Then in about five seconds, the second
2 row with the clarinets turned to look at me. And then — you
3 guessed it — the trumpet section in the third row turned
4 around to stare at me! And then I did what I probably
5 shouldn't have done. I turned around and looked at the wall!
6 The whole class burst out laughing! Everyone except Mr.
7 Hughes! He did not find that funny at all. Instead, he ordered
8 me to the office.
9   So here I am, waiting in the principal's office. I sure hope
10 he has a better sense of humor than Mr. Hughes!

99. Dry Mouth — It's a Symptom!

(Girl or Guy)

1   The worst thing I ever did was take this dumb health
2 class. Because now that I know the things I know, life will
3 never be the same! I miss the days when I thought I was a
4 normal, healthy kid. Why did we have to go over the
5 diseases section anyway? Why couldn't we have skipped
6 through half the book like we do in math class?

7   Who knew that this horrible dry mouth feeling I have
8 could be the symptom of something serious and deadly?
9 And the fact that my hands get sweaty and clammy. That's
10 just another sign. What I really can't ignore are the chills I
11 get at random times. It's like my body is just screaming,
12 "Hey, dummy, something's wrong with you!"

13   But no one will take me seriously. My mom says there
14 is absolutely nothing wrong with me. Well, thank *you,* Mrs.
15 I'm-Not-a-Doctor. What do *you* know? I guess I missed it
16 when you got your medical degree! I tried to show her the
17 diseases that I most likely could have in the book, but she
18 just laughed. That's right. She laughed! What kind of
19 mother laughs at her child's most certain deadly illness?

20   So I asked my teacher about it. Guess what? *She* sure
21 didn't laugh! OK, she may have smiled a lot ... and she may
22 have told me to take my seat ... and then I *did* see her
23 texting something that was clearly cracking her up ... but
24 whatever! Adults have been wrong before. Just because
25 they're older doesn't mean they know *everything.*

1   I just ask you to do one thing: When I collapse and go
2   into a coma, please make sure that you tell my mom and
3   Mrs. Riley, *"I told you so!"*

100. I Am Not Drinking That!

(Girl or Guy)

1 Did you know that the water you are drinking may have
2 once been in someone's toilet? That's right! The same water
3 that flushes down the drain with "you know what" might be
4 sloshing around in your mouth right now! Isn't that
5 disgusting? Why has no one ever told me this before?

6 I guess I never stopped to think about the fact that we
7 have the same water on this earth year after year. It's not
8 like we make more. So the same water that George
9 Washington watered his cherry tree with could be the same
10 water that we use to water our lawn! How crazy is that! I
11 mean, think about the water cycle, people! It's all just a big
12 circle.

13 But back to what's in your mouth. Or rather, what's in
14 *my* mouth. Now that I've figured this out, there is *no* way
15 I'm ever drinking water again. No way! It's like when I found
16 my dog drinking out of the toilet! I thought that was the
17 grossest thing ever. Well, clearly it wasn't! This is by far the
18 worst thing that could ever happen.

19 I know they have water treatment plants, but come on!
20 Are we really supposed to believe that they can get all that
21 nastiness out? I see the particles of stuff floating in my
22 water! Dad says it's just lime in the water, but what if it's
23 not? What if it's *tiny pieces of toilet paper?* Oh my gosh! I
24 think I'm going to be sick!

25 All I know is from here on out, it's bottled water *only* for
26 me! That's the only way I'm drinking water. Wait a minute
27 ... where does the bottled water come from? Oh no!

101. Cat-tastrophe

(Girl or Guy)

1   I really don't understand why I am the one having to
2 suffer when what happened was completely *not* my fault.
3 Just because Mittens is *my* cat doesn't mean that I control
4 what she does! In fact, *no one* can control what she does.
5 She's a little demon cat. And I'm really mad at her! But
6 what can I do? Number one, she's a cat. It's not like I can
7 ground her. And number two, she's oh so cute!
8   Look at that face. So sweet. So innocent. It's not like
9 she probably *meant* to push my phone into the toilet. Well,
10 actually she *did* mean to do that. She does things like that
11 all the time to get my attention. But it's not like she *knows*
12 it's bad. OK, maybe she *does* know it's bad because she
13 always darts off the minute she does something like that.
14 But come on. She's a cat. It's not like she knows how much
15 it costs to replace a phone! And if she knew it was going to
16 hurt me, she would never have done it. My cat *loves* me!
17 That's why she likes getting my attention. So how can I be
18 mad at her for something like that?
19   But Mom and Dad are acting like I shoved the thing in
20 the toilet myself! They're refusing to get me a new one. It's
21 not fair at all! They say I should've had the lid down like I
22 could've known she was going to do that. That's like me
23 saying to Dad, "You should've known that car was going to
24 rear-end you, and so you should've gone another way!"
25 Don't they see? An accident is an accident! What's that old
26 saying? "Hindsight is twenty-twenty"? Well, of course I
27 wished I had the lid down! But I didn't. And I wished that
28 my cat didn't love me so much ... OK, maybe I don't wish

1   that ...
2   All I know is that now my phone won't turn on, my cat
3   is still cute, and my parents are mean.

102. Not Gonna Make It

(Guy)

1   I am so tired of making plans with my friend Adrian,
2 because every time I do, he bails on me at the last minute.
3 I don't even know why he bothers to set stuff up with me. I
4 always think this will be the time we will get to hang out.
5 Maybe play some video games or watch movies. I used to
6 even have Mom buy extra snacks. But now I know better.
7 He's done it so many times that if he actually did show up,
8 I'd be surprised. Sometimes I even double-book myself
9 because I know it's never going to happen.

10   I'd take it personally but the guy is just a major
11 homebody. I seriously wonder if he ever leaves the house
12 besides going to school. And he's the one that always
13 makes the plans. Not me. If he was trying to ditch me as a
14 friend, he wouldn't even bother. But I don't think that's it. I
15 think he really wants to hang out, but he just can't seem to
16 go through with it, for some reason.

17   It's hard not to take it personally, though. I mean, a guy
18 can only take so much rejection. I try not to let it get to me.
19 But it's really frustrating. And let's be honest, it's rude.
20 Even if his intentions are good, his actions stink! I don't
21 want to be mad at him, but sometimes I just can't help it.
22 The last time he bailed, I didn't talk to him for two whole
23 days!

24   I guess maybe I just need to tell him no from now on
25 when he tries to set something up. That way I won't be let
26 down and he won't have to bail. Maybe if I keep telling him
27 I have other plans, he'll actually try harder to finally hang
28 out with me.

103. Why Would My Mom Do That to Me?

(Guy)

1   So I know I'm still young and I have my whole life ahead
2   of me and that there will be lots of things that will be *far*
3   worse than what I've gone through so far ... but seriously?
4   Did my mom really think that a *rat tail* was the way to go
5   when I was in first grade? It's *so* humiliating to go back
6   through the yearbooks and see how awful I looked.

7   Want to know what she did to me in second grade? A
8   mohawk. A really tall, really stiff mohawk. I look like a
9   freak! The spikes look like they could seriously hurt
10 somebody. I'm surprised they even let me go to school that
11 way!

12 Third grade isn't any better. She actually put a colored
13 stripe down the side of my head. Like a skunk! Only it
14 wasn't white, it was bright purple. I can't imagine what the
15 teacher thought when I walked into class that way. No
16 wonder I was always getting into trouble. I looked like a
17 mini-biker!

18 I know my mom thinks she was being the cool mom.
19 Letting me do things that other moms wouldn't. I may have
20 even thought it was cool at the time. But I was just a kid.
21 A stupid little kid. She should've known better! She
22 should've stopped me. She definitely should *not* have
23 encouraged me!

24 The absolute worst was fourth grade. It's embarrassing
25 to even say it. I actually had a *mullet*. The whole "business
26 in the front, party in the back" hairdo! Who *does* that? I'm

1   just glad that I'm old enough and smart enough now to have
2   *normal* haircuts. If I'm lucky, once I get through middle
3   school and high school, no one will even remember the
4   freaky kid I was back then!

About the Author

This is Rebecca Young's ninth drama book for teens. Many of the monologues and plays she writes have been inspired by real-life family or friend events — you'll have to guess which ones!

For many years, Rebecca wrote and directed drama for middle school and high school students for her church. She cofounded a Christian acting group called One Voice. It was a dream of hers to combine writing, acting, and helping youth.

Rebecca currently works in a totally "non-dramatic" profession as a Systems Analyst at Central Bank in Lexington, Kentucky. She has a Bachelor of Arts degree in Communications/Marketing from the University of Kentucky. (But she's not one of the crazy UK basketball fans that you see on TV — don't tell anyone!)

She lives in Kentucky with her three daughters, Heather, Kristina, and Ashley, and her son-in-law, Chris. To round out the family, she has two cats who basically rule the house.

Whether you are an actor or a writer, she suggests this anonymous quote as a daily mantra: "You aren't finished when you lose; you are finished when you quit."

Never give up hope.

Order Form

Meriwether Publishing Ltd.
PO Box 7710
Colorado Springs, CO 80933-7710
Phone: 800-937-5297 Fax: 719-594-9916
Website: www.meriwether.com

Please send me the following books:

_____ **103 Monologues for Middle School Actors** **$17.95**
#BK-B355
by Rebecca Young
More winning comedy and dramatic characterizations

_____ **102 Monologues for Middle School Actors** **$17.95**
#BK-B327
by Rebecca Young
Including comedy and dramatic monologues

_____ **101 Monologues for Middle School Actors** **$16.95**
#BK-B303
by Rebecca Young
Including duologues and triologues

_____ **Famous Fantasy Character Monologs** **$16.95**
#BK-B286
by Rebecca Young
Starring the Not-So-Wicked Witch and more

_____ **102 Great Monologues #BK-B315** **$16.95**
by Rebecca Young
A versatile collection of monologues and duologues for student actors

_____ **Ten-Minute Plays for** **$17.95**
Middle School Performers #BK-B305
by Rebecca Young
Plays for a variety of cast sizes

_____ **More Ten-Minute Plays for** **$17.95**
Middle School Performers #BK-B319
by Rebecca Young and Ashley Gritton
Plays for a variety of cast sizes

**These and other fine Meriwether Publishing books are available at
your local bookstore or direct from the publisher. Prices subject to
change without notice. Check our website or call for current prices.**

Name: _____ email:_____

Organization name: _____

Address: _____

City: _____ State: _____

Zip: _____ Phone: _____

❑ **Check enclosed**

❑ **Visa / MasterCard / Discover / Am. Express #** _____

Signature: _____ *Expiration date:* _____ / _____ *CVV code:* _____
(required for credit card orders)

Colorado residents: Please add 3% sales tax.
Shipping: Include $3.95 for the first book and 75¢ for each additional book ordered.

❑ *Please send me a copy of your complete catalog of books and plays.*